Praise for *How To Be REALLY Productive*

'Deeply practical and soul-searching. Grace is a true Productivity Ninja and this book will challenge you to think differently about your work... and probably your life, too!'

Graham Allcott, author of How to be a Productivity Ninja

'As someone who seems to be constantly juggling people, deadline, projects and tasks and very often feeling overwhelmed as a result, this book cuts through the clutter – literally. Simple, practical tips that help with mindset and busyness, this book helps you get out of overwhelm and into being truly productive.'

Jenny Flintoft, Business and Leadership Consultant, Facilitator and Speaker

'I've read a lot of productivity books and Grace's book is the one I'll be recommending above all others. A practical guide to being productive in an increasingly busy world. It uses real examples which will strike a chord with anyone from those woefully unproductive to more experienced productivity geeks like myself.'

Richard Tubb, IT Business Expert

'If you ever wondered why work and life seem to just pass by, you should read this book. Grace takes you on a road to get more out of your life and helps you think through the tough questions about being productive.'

Fokke Kooistra, Productivity Ninja, Editor of Productive! Magazine, *Netherlands*

'Grace simply gets it – she speaks to me, calms me down and helps me to be really productive. Buy this book, and don't forget your highlighter pen!'

Amanda Alexander PCC, Talent Development Coach, Regional Director, Forward Ladies

'An easy read with some real gems I could implement instantly to add meaning, momentum and a sense of control in my life.'

Susie Kong, Airline Programme Manager

'Ever wished someone could pull together all the great wisdom on effectiveness out there and put it one place? I have, often – so I'm delighted to see that is exactly what Grace has done with this handy book. Drawing together the best bits from books like *The Chimp Paradox* and *The Advantage*, also the latest research, TED Talks and many more sources, Grace has provided a one-stop shop for everything we need to know to be more effective. Filled with practical tips and space for personal reflection and activity, this book challenges us to get into a better frame of mind for being brilliant, and shows us how to get there.'

Helen Frewin, Talent Director, Totem Consulting

'Grace's tips are the kind you can use in ~~~~~~~~ ~~e and get real results.'

liams, Author of Screw Work, Let's Play

'Practical answers to managing productivity – a quirky journey of sound theories, engaging stories and top tips inviting self-reflection to find your very own achievable work–life balance.'

Mairead Minto, Talent Development Manager

'So much advice on time and productivity leaves you with the nagging sense that while the advice is good, it's really for naturally organised types. This book is different: Grace helps you get clear on the hidden gremlins getting in the way of getting things done, and shows you smart, practical ways to remove overwhelm and obstacles to finding time – without changing who you are. The productivity book for real humans.'

Marianne Cantwell, author of Be a Free Range Human

'Grace understands what productivity is all about. It's about achieving happiness and a life you really want for yourself. If you love her articles from the *Productive! Magazine*, you should definitely get her book and achieve productivity which will take your life to a whole new level.'

Michael Sliwinski, CEO and Founder of Nozbe, Chief Editor of Productive! Magazine

'Full of practical suggestions, hints and tips to get the most out of your busy schedule. I guarantee that you'll keep coming back to this book for a refresher course in how to maintain balance in your life.'

June Dennis, Head of the University of Wolverhampton Business School

'What a great use of time: consider this an investment in your "more productive self!" Lots of pragmatic advice, plus easy yet meaningful practice and reflection opportunities. You'll be thinking differently about time and productivity when you're done.'

Kristen Pressner, Global HR executive, International Speaker on Women in Leadership

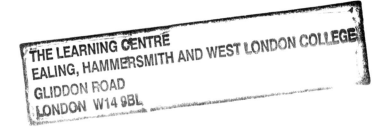

How To Be REALLY Productive

PEARSON

At Pearson, we believe in learning – all kinds of learning for all kinds of people. Whether it's at home, in the classroom or in the workplace, learning is the key to improving our life chances.

That's why we're working with leading authors to bring you the latest thinking and best practices, so you can get better at the things that are important to you. You can learn on the page or on the move, and with content that's always crafted to help you understand quickly and apply what you've learned.

If you want to upgrade your personal skills or accelerate your career, become a more effective leader or more powerful communicator, discover new opportunities or simply find more inspiration, we can help you make progress in your work and life.

Pearson is the world's leading learning company. Our portfolio includes the Financial Times and our education business, Pearson International.

Every day our work helps learning flourish, and wherever learning flourishes, so do people.

To learn more, please visit us at **www.pearson.com/uk**

How To Be REALLY Productive

Achieving clarity and getting results in a world where work never ends

Grace Marshall

PEARSON

Harlow, England • London • New York • Boston • San Francisco • Toronto • Sydney
Auckland • Singapore • Hong Kong • Tokyo • Seoul • Taipei • New Delhi
Cape Town • São Paulo • Mexico City • Madrid • Amsterdam • Munich • Paris • Milan

PEARSON EDUCATION LIMITED
Edinburgh Gate
Harlow CM20 2JE
United Kingdom
Tel: +44 (0)1279 623623
Web: www.pearson.com/uk

First published 2015 (print and electronic)

ISBN: 978-1-292-08383-4 (print)
      978-1-292-08385-8 (PDF)
      978-1-292-08384-1 (eText)
      978-1-292-08386-5 (ePub)

British Library Cataloguing-in-Publication Data
A catalogue record for the print edition is available from the British Library

Library of Congress Cataloging-in-Publication Data
A catalog record for the print edition is available from the Library of Congress

Marshall, Grace.
  How to be really productive : achieving clarity and getting results
in a world where work never ends / Grace Marshall. — 1 Edition.
    pages cm
  Includes bibliographical references and index.
  ISBN 978-1-292-08383-4 (pbk.)
  1. Labor productivity.   2. Work.   I. Title.
  HD57.M26 2015
  650.1—dc23
                                        2015030086
10 9 8 7 6 5 4 3 2 1
19 18 17 16 15

Text design by Design Deluxe
Cover design by Two Associates

Print edition typeset in 9.5pt Mundo Sans Pro by 76
Print edition printed in Great Britain by Henry Ling Ltd, at the Dorset Press, Dorchester, Dorset

NOTE THAT ANY PAGE CROSS REFERENCES REFER TO THE PRINT EDITION

CONTENTS

ABOUT THE AUTHOR

Grace Marshall is head coach and chief encourager at Grace-Marshall.com, author of *21 Ways to Manage the Stuff That Sucks Up Your Time* and a Productivity Ninja with Think Productive, one of the world's leading productivity training companies.

She believes in changing the world, one conversation at a time – whether that's behind a microphone, at the kitchen table, in workshops, with clients, over a cuppa or on the page. If it helps people find ways of doing their best work, living their best life and defining success according to what matters most, she's up for it.

Grace admits that she's not a naturally organised person. Her passion for productivity began when she got fed up of saying, 'I haven't got enough time'.

She lives in Stafford – somewhere in the middle of the UK – with her husband and their two children. When she's not working (and sometimes when she is), you will probably find her surrounded by people, books, music, board games, faith and food – possibly even all at once.

AUTHOR'S ACKNOWLEDGEMENTS

They say it takes a village to raise a child and the birth of this 'baby' feels the same. So many voices have spoken into this book and made this happen, many more than I can name here, but, as imperfection isn't a good enough reason not to start, here is an imperfect and incomplete list of those I would like to thank from the bottom of my heart.

Graham Allcott at Think Productive and Steve Temblett at Pearson for the conversations that started this particular journey.

Amanda Alexander for the relentless cheerleading, mind-monkey wrestling and expert coaching through the crazy wilderness of writing, working and everything else. I hope I haven't put you off writing your book!

June Dennis, Jenny Flintoft, Katy Bateson, Susie Kong, Fokke Kooistra, Richard Tubb, Jim Hetherton, Caroline Ferguson, Sian-Elin Flint-Freel for your care, thoughtfulness and insight, taking the time in between your own juggling to road-test the rough draft and help me to shape the final book.

Clients, readers, friends and colleagues – your questions brought me here and continue to fuel me more than you know. Keep them coming...

Ruth, Rebekah, Eve, Wendy, Jenny M. and Jenny J. for taking the time to share your thoughts and stories with me, particularly for this book.

Rob Archer, Penny Pullen, Eveliina Lindell, Jennie H. K., Marianne Cantwell, Josie George, Jacob Mahal and my fellow Productivity Ninjas – thanks for the geek-out conversations. May there be more to come!

Some days a writer's life is exactly how you imagine: eating cake, drinking tea, inhaling caffeine and typing away to Nina Simone – thanks to the wonderful staff at The Bean Encounter – my writing cave – for making that happen.

Grante, Oliver and Catherine, my best reason ever. Thank you for loving the best out of me and living with the rest.

PUBLISHER'S ACKNOWLEDGEMENTS

We are grateful to the following for permission to reproduce copyright material:

Figures

Figure on page 26 after *The Seven Habits of Highly Effective People*, Simon & Schuster (Stephen R. Covey, 2005).

Text

Text on page 58, from Helen Routledge, Head of Design and Production, Totem Learning Ltd.; text on page 78 from Caroline Ferguson. Mindset Trainer; text on pages 144–5 with permission from MOO (moo.com)

Picture Credits

The publisher would like to thank the following for their kind permission to reproduce their photographs on pages xii-xiii:

Pearson Education Ltd: 123rf.com; dandoo, Shutterstock; pockygallery, Shutterstock; Sanjay Charadva. Pearson India Education Services Pvt. Ltd.

Lightbulb image used throughout: Somchai Som, Shutterstock

All other images © Pearson Education

Every effort has been made to trace the copyright holders and we apologise in advance for any unintentional omissions. We would be pleased to insert the appropriate acknowledgement in any subsequent edition of this publication.

In some instances we have been unable to trace the owners of copyright material, and we would appreciate any information that would enable us to do so.

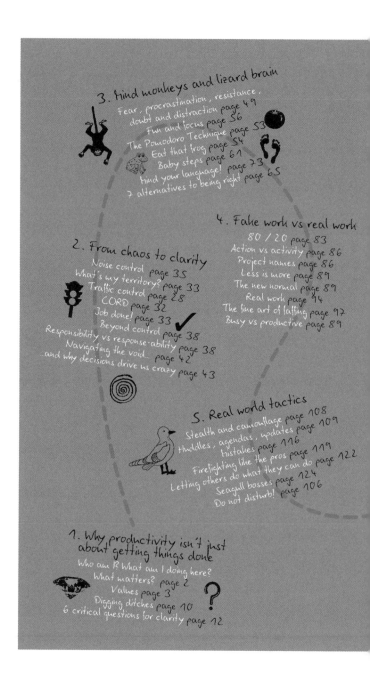

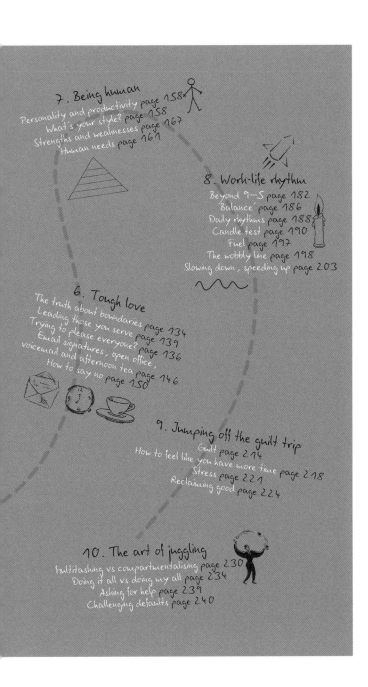

Chapter 1

Why productivity isn't just about getting things done

What's the difference between time spent and time well spent? Between brilliant productivity and just getting things done? Yes, it's satisfying to tick things off a list. Yes, there are days when just surviving is a rewarding achievement. But, over the longer term, it is not enough to just go through the motions.

What makes a day productive is not just the number of tasks we tick off a 'to do' list. It's the satisfaction, the sense of achievement and progress, and the knowledge that what we do matters. It's waking up looking forward to doing our best work and having fun doing it. It's coming home feeling satisfied and enjoying life outside of work. It's about experience as well as achievement. It's about the quality of our life at work, as well as the work itself.

In this book we will explore the things that get in the way – the chaos, the noise, the procrastination, the interruptions, the crazy deadlines, the last-minute boss and much, much more – but, before we dive into the nitty gritty, I want to challenge you first to think beyond survival and simply getting things done. What would it look like to thrive, to do your best work, have fun doing it and have a life outside of work?

True productivity is satisfaction in a world where the work never ends. Excitement without exhaustion. Opportunity without overwhelm. It's the ability to give our best in any situation and to keep giving our best. To be on fire with passion and purpose without burning out. To work, rest and play without feeling guilty. To enjoy the crazy times without going crazy and the calm times without getting bored.

How do we get there? We need to start with meaning, purpose and joy.

Meaning

Does what I'm doing matter? More importantly, does it matter to me?

We all need to know that what we are doing matters. That we are not just cranking some big hamster wheel, churning out stuff for the sake of it. A while ago, some good friends of mine worked in the R&D laboratory of a technology company, where the working environment was great, the pay was pretty good and the team got on like a house on fire. But the projects they worked on kept getting shelved – their creations never went to market because of decisions being made higher up. However good the pay, the job, the team, the environment and the perks, it did not make up for the fact that their work had no meaning. Their efforts were pointless.

What's more, we need to know that what we are doing matters to us. Time feels productive only when what we spend it on is personally meaningful. And what is meaningful is highly subjective and individual. Doing what we think we 'should' do – or what others define as successful – is not enough.

In my early graduate days, I found myself in a job where the highlight of my week was when I made a difference to someone else's day – when I helped a colleague solve a computer issue that had nothing to do with my job, when I made someone else's life easier. Success became measured by how happy other people were with me, not by how well I was doing the job, and making decisions was a nightmare because, essentially, it became an exercise in mind reading rather than taking the initiative. The work was very worthy and contributed to a great cause, but it was not meaningful to me. It did not grab me by the heart and compel me to action, because it did not honour my values.

Values

Values are who we are. Not who we would like to be, not who we think we should be, but who we are in our lives, right now. They are the essence of who we are, what brings us to life and what holds the greatest meaning in life for us. They serve as a compass, pointing out what it means to be true to ourselves. When we honour our values on a regular and consistent basis, life is good and fulfilling. When we suppress, neglect or violate our values, life becomes pointless, frustrating and soul destroying.

One of my core values is helping people. When I realised that there was a mismatch between my values and the job role and environment in which I was working, I realised that it did not matter how good I got at doing the job, I would never give it my best. No matter how hard I worked, I would never be able to do my best work and I would never be truly satisfied with the work I did.

What are your core values?

Take a moment to think about what your values might be. Here are some of the questions I ask my coaching clients, to help them identify their core values:

- What is important to you?
- What do you believe in?
- What drives you?
- What must you have in your life, or a part of you dies?

Think of peak moments in your life, times that were especially rewarding or poignant, and answer the following questions:

- What was happening?
- Who was present and what was going on?
- What were the values that were being honoured in that moment?

Take a look at times when you were upset, distressed, angry or frustrated and answer the following questions:

- What was happening?
- How did you feel?
- What values were being violated or supressed?

What are your top three values? Rank them in order, then score each one out of 10: how well are you honouring or expressing these values in your life right now? Use the box below to start capturing your core values. You can come back to it when something else comes to mind – or when you want to revisit or review your values.

My core values

	Score
1.	
2.	
3.	

- What's working well? Which parts of your work and life are well aligned with your values?

- What's not aligned? Is there anything that violates one of your core values?

- What changes could you explore? How could you live and work more in line with your values?

Purpose

We all know what it's like to be on purpose. When we know where we're heading with unfaltering focus and we will move heaven and earth to get there. We might have experienced it in a moment, when driving a child to A&E, or trying to get a child to sleep, for that matter. Perhaps when we are faced with a crisis or a deadline. A 'now or never' moment.

Purpose gives us a direction to aim for and fuel to get us there. But what keeps us fired up and makes us deeply satisfied that what we do matters, that what we are working towards counts, is when that purpose lasts beyond the moment – beyond the crisis, beyond keeping the client or keeping your job, beyond paying the bills and staying alive.

It all starts with the question 'Why?', as Simon Sinek explains in one of the most popular TED talks of all time:[1] 'Why' is how the greatest leaders inspire action; why 250,000 people showed up to hear Dr Martin Luther King give his 'I have a dream' speech; why people stood in line for six hours to buy an iPhone when it first came out; and why the Wright brothers took flight before other teams who were better qualified and better funded – because they believed in what they were doing. They were working towards a dream that they believed in, rather than just a pay cheque, recognition or obligation.

How purposeful are your current projects? Why are you in business, why does your organisation exist – and how much do you believe in it? What is your sense of life purpose that goes beyond your job, your title or your obligations? How clear are you about why you do what you do?

The deeper the connection between what's inside of us, personally (our values, our beliefs, our identity), and the bigger thing that we are contributing to outside of ourselves (our calling, our cause, our why), the stronger our purpose. Simon Sinek calls this 'inside-out communication' – when we start with why, we speak directly to our limbic system, the lizard brain that drives our strongest decision making (more on that later) – rather than just our rational, logical brain that tells us what we **should** be doing. It's the reason why there are some things we almost cannot stop ourselves from doing, whilst for others we have to summon the energy and cajole ourselves. When we start with 'why', the 'what' and the 'how'.

Purpose gives us direction: it helps us distinguish between activity and action, from going through the motions to actually making progress. Purpose gives us drive, it's what makes the difference between dragging ourselves out of bed to work and tearing ourselves away from it (and remembering to eat and sleep). Purpose also gives us determination to go beyond our comfort zone, resilience to fall down and keep getting up again, and the grit to press through the tough times when we know that we are contributing to something bigger than ourselves. Purpose brings out the best in us and gives us the deepest satisfaction from our work.

How on purpose are you right now?

Joy

What is productivity without joy? Empty drudgery, an interminable chore. Without joy, productivity becomes exhausting – a continual striving for something that is always beyond reach. How much we do becomes the measure of our self-worth. The reward of achievement becomes a fleeting sense of satisfaction followed swiftly by 'what's next?'.

I believe that, as human beings, we are designed to derive joy from working – to feel good about putting our effort into something and seeing it grow into something more. There is something incredibly soul-satisfying about getting to the end of the day and feeling what I can only describe as 'good knackered' – when you are naturally tired and also charged, and it feels good. Like when your body has had a good workout and you feel more alive than before. When the doing has done you good, as well as the good you have done. When you experience joy in the process of working – and the times when you are not working – as well as the fruits of your labour.

Celebrating success

What we focus on grows. Research suggests we actually have three times more positive experiences than negative, but two main tendencies keep us from experiencing, extending and expanding our joy: the negativity bias – that our minds have a natural tendency to linger on and give more weight to negative experiences; and habituation – when things become so familiar that they lose their power to amaze and captivate us.[2]

One way to counter this is to focus deliberately on what's going well. To intentionally savour and relive the positive experiences by writing them down, capturing them and sharing them.

Celebrate what you want to see more of, and don't just keep it to yourself, share it with someone who cares.

Research has found that:

'discussing positive experiences leads to heightened well-being, increased overall life satisfaction and even more energy... sharing our joy increases joy. Telling people about our happiness has far greater benefits than just remembering it or writing it down for ourselves.'[3]

It turns out that this increases the well-being of those around us, too. That joy can be contagious or, as Nobel Peace Prize-winner Albert Schweitzer, said:

'Happiness is the only thing that multiplies when you share it.'

Here are some simple ways you can practise celebrating success:

- Keep a daily journal, gratitude list or 'ta-da' list.

- Share your daily, weekly or monthly wins with a coach, mentor or friend.

- Start each team meeting with 'what's your good news?' (or make it part of your dinner-table conversation).

- Have a 'celebrations' board in your office.

- Set up a 'champagne moments' folder in your email to store testimonials, positive feedback and thank you emails.

- Use a service such as **idonethis.com** to keep track of your daily wins.

Successful living

How do you define success: by results or by actions? Results are tangible and easy to define: a project completed, a new client on the books, a sale made, a sum of money in the bank, a system implemented, a target hit, another product sold and shipped. And it can be great for motivation: knowing what you get when your actions pay off.

But it can also be demoralising when you're in the middle of taking the actions you need to take, to achieve that success. When you're making call after call, writing email after email, sending invitations, posting blogs, submitting proposals, and they're not translating into results... at least not yet.

The actions you take to achieve your results are vital. Yet, if success is defined purely by results, your actions have no value until they lead to a result. Your motivation hangs on the hope of reaching that goal, otherwise your efforts are for nothing.

The problem with focusing purely on results is that you're a failure until you get that result. And when you do get the result, success is fleeting and momentary. Then it's on to pursuing the next booking or the next client, where you are, yet again, back in the place of pursuing, hoping and wondering if you 'have what it takes'.

But the problem is, feeling like a failure does not help us towards success. It invites us to spend time and energy entertaining doubt and indecision, to go round in circles questioning ourselves and our own abilities. It tempts us to spend hours, days and even weeks researching and obsessing about the competition, devoting our energy and attention to studying their every move, rather than our own.

It makes us desperate for the sale, and we all know well from dating days that desperation does not attract. It puts all our focus on what other people do, rather than what we do – whether the audience smile or frown rather than how we deliver our message, and whether the prospective client says yes or no, rather than the conversations we have, the relationships we build and the work we do giving them a reason to say 'yes'.

And it steals our joy.

Now and again, I catch myself being too focused on results. Even though things have been going really well and I have lots of reasons to be happy, I find myself in a lull in between results and I feel subdued. Not terrible or bad, just a bit muted. I get to the end of what, by all accounts, is a very productive day, take account of everything I have done but, because I haven't put a metaphorical tick in my results box, I feel like there is an itch I haven't quite scratched. I feel dissatisfied, unproductive even.

One evening, in the middle of one of these lulls, I was with a small group of people who knew me well, where we did an exercise of writing down what we saw in each other and then each of us took away a list of our own qualities, attributes and words of encouragement from the rest of the group. At the top of my list were three things: 'A seed sower. An inspiration. A light in the dark.' And it hit me: sowing seeds, inspiring people, shining a light. This is what I do; these are my measures of success. And I had done all of them that day.

Success is something you do, not something you have. How are you doing success?

When I do these things day in, day out, the results come. I know that. (In fact, when I first wrote about this, one result came in just before the post went live – talk about timing!) Plus, when I focus on doing these things, my day is fulfilling. I'm proud of how I have spent my time. I am being successful.

Of course results are important. Setting goals is useful. But, when we define success purely by results, it's always something out there. Something we are aiming for or pining for. Something we want but don't have. When we define success by the actions we take, success becomes a journey rather than a destination. Something we have and something we continue to grow and create. Every day that we take that journey, we are living in success. Now *that* I find motivating. Rocket fuel for actions and results.

Digging ditches

Sometimes the work we do does not look successful at all. As someone who always advocates celebrating successes, this might sound strange: it's not all about the highlights, the celebrations, the ideas that go viral, the launches that sell out, the results that go way beyond your wildest dreams.

We think it is; it's what we hear about, what we cite in great examples, role models and industry leaders. Often, when people ask me, 'How's business?', I feel this pressure to reel off the highlights – achievements, successes and what has gone right, whilst brushing under the table what has flopped, what looks crazy and what I'm still trying to get working.

A while ago, I sent this out on Twitter and, judging by the amount of times it was retweeted, I think it resonated with a lot of people:

'One reason we struggle with insecurity is because we compare our behind-the-scenes with other people's highlight reel.'[4]

The quote came from Steven Furtick, a speaker I was particularly encouraged by at a leadership conference, in a talk he gave about digging ditches. He talked about a biblical story where the kings of Edom, Israel and Judah were leading a campaign to overcome the Moabites and found themselves in a dry and barren land where they could not water their armies. The prophet Elisha gives them a message to 'dig ditches', that the rain would come and fill the land, even though no clouds could be seen. They dug. Rain came. But the digging was not to bring on the rain – God could send the water regardless – it was preparation, so that everything was in place ready for when the rain came.

Sometimes we find ourselves in dry and barren times, when it's hard work and there is no sign of rain. Those are the times when we question our vision, when we are tempted to give up and start looking elsewhere, where the grass is at least growing, let alone greener. But, sometimes that is precisely when we need to dig ditches.

Digging ditches means believing enough in a vision to act on it, even when there are no signs of certainty or success. In fact, the difference between a forecast and a vision is that a forecast is limited to what you can see immediately in front of you, whereas a vision goes beyond the horizon, where nothing is certain and anything is possible.

Not that a forecast gives certainty, either – it just feels safer to react to a forecast than to act towards a vision that (at the moment) can be seen only in your heart. It's having audacious faith. As Furtick put it,

'the difference between a vision and a daydream is the audacity to act and the faith to get started'.

Are you acting on a vision, or just simply following the forecast?

Digging ditches means you put in the hard work now to be ready for the opportunities that are yet to come, rather than waiting for a sign or chasing rainbows. And it goes beyond that first moment of inspiration, which can sometimes seem fleeting or ungrounded. It's the act of putting your stake (or shovel) in the ground and saying I'm going to see this happen. I'm going to work towards this vision. I don't know how it's going to pan out, but I'm going to invest myself and prepare for it, nonetheless.

Digging ditches does not look successful. It can seem pointless, even laughable, especially when you see no sign of rain. Sometimes what we are working on does not look successful or fruitful. There is nothing glamourous about digging ditches. Sometimes it looks like dry and hard work. But it's precisely this work that prepares you, stretches you and grows your capacity to take on, harness and run with the opportunities when they arise, to reap the blessings when the rain comes. Remember Noah?

He looked ridiculous building an ark... until the rain came. Then it made sense. Only with hindsight does digging become obvious.

Digging ditches means your focus is on your behind-the-scenes efforts, rather than staring longingly at other people's highlight reels. That's what I mean when I say it's not all about the successes. It's about the work we put in, before it looks successful, before we see any signs of certainty. It's about what we do behind the scenes that enables anything to happen out front. That is what real business – and real productivity – is about: digging ditches as well as celebrating successes.

Vision

How do you stay purposeful – from the big-picture life purpose to day-by-day focus? I find these six critical questions for clarity from Patrick Lencioni[5] really helpful. While his focus is mainly on large organisations, I have found these questions equally critical for small businesses and individual purpose and vision.

Here they are, with a little rewording for those of us looking from an individual point of view.

1. WHY DO WE EXIST? WHY AM I IN BUSINESS? WHAT IS MY CORE PURPOSE?

My accountant probably would say that the reason for being in business should be to make a profit (he is very old school, bless him). I would disagree. Our core purpose is what gets us out of bed, lights us up inside, keeps us inspired through the rollercoaster ride and rewards us with that immense sense of satisfaction when we work towards it.

For many of the people I've met, worked with and coached, money isn't it. Yes, it plays an essential part in running a healthy business, but there is a deeper 'why' beyond the money. My primary purpose, at its most basic level, is about helping people. Being profitable enables me to keep helping people and growing my business helps me to help more people. It's a simple tweak in perspective that enables me to pursue my business wholeheartedly.

Sometimes our 'why' has nothing to do with what we do. Lencioni gives an example of a paving company that realised its core purpose was not about driveways at all. It was about providing jobs in their community. In fact, if the paving industry went away, they would move onto roofing or something else. That is what motivates them to run a successful business, to do a good job and get paid for it.

For my friend, Sharon, it's about supporting and enabling her son to pursue his tennis career so, for her, business opportunities are only 'fit for purpose' if they allow her to be flexible and meet those commitments.

When we are clear about our core purpose and we stay true to the fundamental reason why we do what we do, it gives us motivation, direction, fuel and fulfilment. What is your 'why'?

2. HOW DO WE BEHAVE? WHAT ARE MY VALUES AND HOW DO I LIVE THEM OUT?

Patrick Lencioni describes a core value as something you're willing to get punished for, and violating it would be like selling your soul. He gave an example of Southwest Airlines, who showed their fun-loving-spirit value in action when a customer complained that there were too many jokes in the safety announcement. Instead of apologising, toning down the humour and assuring that safety would be taken more seriously in future, Southwest replied with a three-worded comment, 'We'll miss you!'.

One of my core values is generosity. That means I give a lot of information away freely, on my blog, in talks and teleseminars and in conversation and, sometimes, some people will take only the free stuff. That's ok, because I know I have even more to give to my clients. It also means I collaborate better than I negotiate!

This is about being you, not all things to all people. When you know what makes you you, and live that out in how you work and the way you do business, your offering becomes much more distinctive and you stand out from the crowd. You operate from a place of strength, working in a way that comes naturally to you. You stand your ground, instead of chasing every possible lead, and you start attracting customers who value what you value, making your work far more rewarding and fun.

My friend Rebekah is a social media consultant who expresses her value of creativity in the vibrant and colourful way she dresses. You will never find her in a suit, but that is precisely why she stands out to the kind of creative, expressive clients she loves to work with – ones that make very expensive handbags, for example!

What are your core values? What do they look like day to day? How do you live them out in the way you do business?

3. WHAT DO WE DO? WHAT DO I DO?

Now that you know your 'why' and your 'how', it's time clarify your 'what', because actions are what, ultimately, makes things happen. What do you actually do? What is the nature of your business or your work? This is the simple 'does what it says on the can' statement.

If you just want to help people, how specifically are you going to choose to do that? What is your stake in the ground that says 'this is what I do'? The clearer you are about your plan of action, the more focused you can be in your implementation. Can you describe what you do clearly and accurately, in a way your prospective clients, networking contacts or a five-year-old can understand?

4. HOW WILL WE SUCCEED? HOW WILL I SUCCEED?

This is your strategy. There are lots of paths to success, and strategy is about choosing yours. Rather than having every detail mapped out, Lencioni suggests having three 'strategic anchors' that inform day-to-day decisions.

For example, Southwest Airlines' strategic anchors are to 'keep fair prices low', 'create fanatically loyal customers' and 'make sure the planes are on time'. So, would they invest in the latest reclining seats or a fancier on-board menu? Well, in all likelihood, that would push their costs and prices higher, so the answer is, probably, no.

On the other hand, my friend Liz runs a cupcake company that is all about bespoke, handmade, delicious, fresh cupcakes. Would she look at getting her cakes mass-manufactured? No. Would she offer to match decorations to a bride's bouquet or make the Superman figure on a six-year-old's cake look just like the birthday boy? Yes.

One of my strategic anchors is building personal relationships. So, given the choice between advertising in a magazine and writing for them, I will go for the writing every time. Given the choice between sponsoring and speaking at an event, I would choose to speak because it gives me a voice and an opportunity to connect with people on a more personal level.

When we are clear on our strategy, it's much easier to distinguish between opportunities and distractions, decide what's important and what's not, make day-to-day decisions and filter down from a myriad of 'all the things I could do' to what you are choosing to focus on and do exceptionally well. What are your strategic anchors?

5. WHAT IS MOST IMPORTANT RIGHT NOW?

When organisations have different teams pursuing different agendas, the result is chaos, frustration and confusion and the effects are demoralising. When individual business owners pursue several different things all at once, the result is frustration, a feeling of being overwhelmed, confusion and, often, 'running around like a headless chicken'.

You can do anything, but not everything, right now. So, what are you going to **focus** on? What is going to make the biggest impact towards your core purpose? What are you choosing to commit to first? What is most important right now?

6. WHO MUST DO WHAT? WHAT MUST I DO?

In an organisation, this is about roles and responsibilities. Now that you have your purpose, your values, your actions, your strategy and your priorities, who is actually going to do what? How clear is everyone about where their individual responsibilities start and finish and what their core focus is right now?

If you are the only one in your business or your team, it's tempting to answer this question with, 'Me – everything,' but defining your role is as beneficial for you, the decision maker, as it is for those to whom you delegate. There are the things you must do, that only you can do, that are key to your business; the 'essential requirements' on your job spec or the big rocks in your business plan. There are the ideals, the nice-to-haves, the icing on the cake. And then there is the occasional 'muck in', like my friend the youth worker who saw that the girls' toilets were overflowing and got

the mop and bucket out. It was not her job, but she mucked in and got it done. If you are the only person in your business, you will probably find yourself mucking in with things you never thought you would be doing but, if you spend all your time there, nobody will be taking care of the big rocks.

This is as much a question of time as it is about team. Whether you are in business by yourself or part of a wider team, the question here is where should I be spending most of my time?

Over to you

My personal productivity vision

1. Why do I do what I do? What is my core purpose?

....

2. What are my values and how do I live them out?

....

3. What do I do? What's my chosen way of achieving my purpose?

....

4. How will I succeed? What are my strategic anchors?

....

5. What is most important right now? What is my focus in this season?

....

6. Who must do what? What must I do? Where should I be spending most of my time?

....

My personal definition of success

Successful living is when I am:

....

Ditches I'm digging right now include:

....

I celebrate everyday success by:

....

Now we know where you want to go, let's start clearing the way through the chaos.

Chapter 2

From chaos to clarity

What is it about chaos that kills our productivity? We all recognise that feeling – when chaos has us stuck, overwhelmed, chasing our tail or frozen to the spot, angry, frustrated or confused, feeling lost or going over the same ground again and again.

Sometimes it's low-level chaos:

> A little nag in the back of your head whilst trying to prepare for a client meeting.

> A few minutes of paper shuffling to find that report you need.

> A flutter of uncertainty as you glance at your inbox, wondering 'is there an email I've forgotten to deal with somewhere in the pile?'.

> A couple of tricky conversations to negotiate.

> A slight panic when you think of the deadline that's approaching on the horizon.

> A missed call here, running a few minutes late there, remembering, at 11:53 pm, that you really ought to book that dentist appointment – and that you've forgotten to call your mother, again.

> A vague feeling of familiarity when you revisit that item on your to-do list that's been stuck there for a while, followed by light relief, with a sprinkling of guilt, when you turn to something that's easier to tick off the list instead.

Sometimes it's complete hair-pulling, brain-melting, stop-the-world-and-let-me-off-**now** chaos:

> When all the conversations and all the projects and all the deadlines all converge into one.

> When you forget your own name, let alone that person whose email you desperately need to find.

> When you're having multiple conversations in your head, on your screen, on multiple screens, and a small voice that says 'where's that file?' or 'what's for dinner?' sends you over the edge.

> When everything takes you by surprise and, the minute you think you've got something nailed, it all changes.

When you feel like there are so many unanswered questions, but you haven't even figured out what the questions are.

When your brain shuts up shop and sets up an automatic reply of 'I know nothing'.

When you can't get to sleep because you keep replaying that conversation with Inland Revenue, and you wake up dreaming that you're texting a colleague to apologise for missing your 2 pm call, only to look in your diary later in the day and find it's scheduled for 1 pm.

When the dread of opening your emails becomes so overwhelming that it spoils your weekend if you don't check it to allay your fears.

When the requests and the work and the interruptions and the fires just keep coming.

When you keep telling yourself 'when': when things slow down; when that event is over; when this project is finished; when I hit this deadline; when I clear that backlog.

When all you want to do is press **stop**, hide in a cave and play Candy Crush because, at least then, you will feel like you know what the heck you're doing!

Where's your chaos?

Not all chaos is the same. What kind of chaos are you dealing with? How many of these can you identify with?

Unfinished business

> **'Chaos comes from decisions that haven't been made.'**
> **EVELIINA LINDELL, PROFESSIONAL ORGANISER[1]**

It starts with something small: a document we put on our desk to read later; a leaflet we might be interested in; an email we're not sure how to respond to. When those little things pile up, they become big things: backlogs, clutter, never-ending to-do lists and overflowing inboxes.

It's not just physical clutter, either. The jobs that stack up in our head create chaos: when you find it hard to switch off; when you're working on one project and the other refuses to leave you alone; when your body leaves work at the end of the day but your brain doesn't – the chances are you have unfinished business.

The predictably unpredictable

This can be anything, from last-minute requests, clients you keep having to chase, bosses who change their minds, colleagues who ask you for help, but don't actually know what they want, trains that get delayed, technology that decides to run slowly just when you have two minutes to grab that document before the meeting, to handouts that get lost in the post.

It's not just work, either. It could be children waking up at 5 am; a last-minute wardrobe disaster; socks that 'don't feel right' when you're rushing children out of the door; when your mother decides to call just at that moment when you're trying to coax the cat down from the fridge, mop up the milk and break up a fight between the kids without burning the spaghetti.

We know they're coming, we just don't know quite how or when – and we haven't decided how we're going to deal with them.

Plot twists and curveballs

Sometimes things don't go to plan. Sometimes plans change. With the best of intentions and planning, we do get hit with genuine curveballs. Things we didn't plan for, things we couldn't have planned for and, often, things we have little or no control over: when the company announces a restructure; when tax rules change; when ill health hits or when your bank account gets frozen; when a landslide diverts all trains, or the school closes because of a boiler failure; when your boiler decides to flood the kitchen or your coffee flask leaks all over your bag.

The hardest thing about this type of chaos is the simultaneous loss of control and the urge to take control somehow. You feel responsible for finding a solution and powerless to stop the problem from occurring in the first place.

Noise

Sometimes chaos comes from noise: too much going on; too many voices; too many emails; too many distractions and interruptions demanding your attention.

These are the days when you know you've been busy, but have no idea what you've actually achieved. Days when a piece of work takes you 10 times longer because you keep getting interrupted. When everyone and everything in the office, on your desk, in your inbox and in your head seems to be demanding your attention all at once.

The void

Sometimes our source of chaos is not noisy at all. In fact, it's almost the opposite of noise.

It's the void of uncertainty – that massive project you've committed to, the role you've taken on, that deadline you've just agreed to – where you know you have a responsibility to deliver, but you have no idea what the work will actually look like, let alone where to begin.

In the face of uncertainty, our minds try to fill the void. With questions. With scenarios. With projections good and bad. With possibilities – infinite possibilities. And ideas. And fears. In the absence of knowing, we imagine. And, sometimes, that can be far more chaotic than any reality.

Time travellers

Then there's the chaos that doesn't even exist – at least, not right now, in this moment. This is the chaos that comes from hanging onto the past or worrying about the future.

How often do you find yourself replaying conversations, rethinking decisions, rewriting emails in your head, dissecting that meeting that didn't go so well, worrying about the deadline you have coming up, while wondering what to cook for tea?

Reflecting, reviewing and planning can be useful, of course, but, when it becomes dwelling and worrying, it's surprising how much space this can take up in our heads.

The runaway train

Sometimes, chaos comes from the sheer speed that we are travelling. Things are happening so fast that we don't have time to think or stop – have you ever tried to jump off a moving train?

The days when you rocket from one thing to another, screeching round corners and sweeping people along with you: when it works, it's exhilarating – an achievement in itself. But, when it doesn't, and you veer off course, the crash can be spectacular. It's a job in itself just keeping the train on the tracks.

At this speed, everything feels chaotic. The unexpected and the expected. The big stuff and the little stuff. There is no time to stop and think. In fact, 'I haven't got time' has probably become your mantra.

Chaos kills our productivity when it scatters our focus, steals our energy and sends us spinning in a hundred different directions. It convinces us that there's no time to stop, let alone enjoy, the journey; that there is no point because we can't control it all, anyway; that the only option is just to keep kicking our legs as fast as we can and hope that we don't drown.

But what if we have more control – and need less control – than we think? What if, instead of attempting to control it all, we can create our own oceans of calm in a world of chaos, ride the waves without losing ourselves, and let life take our breath away without killing us?

What we really need is not control, but clarity, to do our best work and live our best lives from the midst of the chaos.

Creating clarity: what's your territory?

Do you ever have the feeling that you're chasing your own thoughts around your head? Try and pinpoint a thought and it seems to run away and spiral into several other thoughts. Try to work out a problem and, the more you think about it, the worse it seems to get. Try and focus on one thing and several other jobs start nagging at you.

> 'Your mind is for having ideas, not for holding them.'
> DAVID ALLEN, AUTHOR OF *GETTING THINGS DONE* [2]

The more you try and keep in your head, the less headspace you have to think with.

It's really hard to gain perspective when everything is in your head and you can't see the wood for the trees. When everything is close up, in your face, demanding your attention. It's also harder to separate your thoughts and your feelings, your reality from your fear, evidence from imagination: fear and difficulty often can appear larger in your head.

Step 1 Identify the chaos: what's on your mind?

The first step to navigating chaos is to get it out of your head and capture it on paper (or a screen), where you can see it all in one place and start to make sense of it, instead of perpetually chasing thoughts around your head.

Do it now. Go and grab a pen and paper or, better still, a stack of Post-it® Notes, and ask yourself, 'What's on my mind?'. Then write. Write down everything – things you need to do, things you are concerned about, things you are trying to remember, projects you have on the go, errands you need to run, people you need to call, ideas you have knocking around your head. Simply do a brain dump and empty your head.

Step 2 Identify the territory: worry vs. work

Not everything you worry about is within your control. Not everything you write down will have something you can do about it. Sometimes our greatest chaos comes from feeling obligated without being in control: having a responsibility over a situation without the capability or capacity to do something about it. We need to separate the worry from the work.

An exercise I use often with my clients is Stephen Covey's Circles of Concern and Influence.[3]

- On a large sheet of paper, draw two circles – one inside the other.

- For each item you have written down, ask yourself, 'Can I do something about this?'

- If the answer is no, put it in the outer circle. This is what Stephen Covey calls the circle of concern. These are the things that may impact you, but you have no control over.

- If the answer is yes, put it in the inner circle. This is your circle of influence. These are the things you can do something about.

Take a look at the overall picture. How much of your focus is in your circle of concern? How much of your time and attention is taken up by worry over things that are beyond your control?

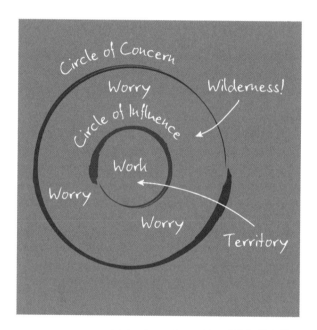

Here's your choice: you can choose to wander aimlessly in the vast wilderness of worry (and there will be plenty to keep you busy there) or you can focus on the work and claim it as your territory. The choice is yours.

Step 3 Identify the work

Now take a look at the inner circle. For each thing you have written down, ask yourself, 'Am I clear what I need to do here?'.

If you have written something like, 'Sort website' or 'Charlie's behaviour', it might be within your sphere of influence but, if you haven't identified what you need to do about it, then it will remain a worry rather than something you can actually work on.

To identify the work, ask yourself, 'What do I need to do about this?' There might be several things that come to mind. Make a note of them. If you are using Post-it Notes, put each thing on a separate note. Then ask yourself, 'What's the first thing I need to do about this?'. Then make sure that that one is at the top of the pile and is the one you can see when you look at your circle of influence.

Repeat this until everything in your circle of influence is a clear action that you can take. Now you have your work.

Clarity in the work

What makes today's world of work particularly chaotic?

1. **The work never ends.** The days come and go, but there is always more to be done. More calls you can make, more research you can do, more errands to run, ideas to pursue, people to connect with, leads to follow up on, more emails that land in your inbox, more requests, more opportunities, more horizons to explore, more challenges to meet, more targets to break...

2. **Work doesn't form an orderly queue.** Work arrives at different times, in different ways and progresses at different speeds. Our job is not just to do the work. It's to work out the work – to define the work, to choose the work, to manage the work, to juggle the work...

3. **Life doesn't stop when you work.** Of course, it's not just the work. It's the life outside of work – from everyday chores like taking out the bin and buying toothpaste, to things you keep meaning to get round to, like making that doctor's appointment, calling

your friend or writing your will, to big things such as moving house, getting married and choosing schools, and fun things, like seeing friends, building kit cars, band practice, marathon training or going on holiday – and, even, simple things such as eating and sleeping! All this needs to happen too, in between, around and alongside the work.

Sometimes it feels like everything is moving in different directions, waiting for a spectacular crash. At other times, it's gridlock. Nothing is moving. There's traffic, there's noise, it's stressful, but nothing seems to be moving forward.

That is when we need some traffic control.

Traffic control

Managing workflow is a bit like traffic control. If you let everything run in every direction, there is chaos. Nothing gets done, everything goes crazy and you are likely to see some spectacular crashes.

Think of all the things you have on your plate right now – tasks, projects, errands, chores, ideas, nags, reminders – at work, at home, in your personal life, your social life...

How many things do you have on your to-do list and on your radar right now? How much of it is on red, where you're stuck and don't know how to move forward? How much is on amber, where you're waiting for someone else, something else or even on your decision before you can move forward? How much is on green, where you're good to go?

RED: WHAT'S STUCK?

What's stuck but still on your radar? Maybe you've hit a dead end. Maybe it's not quite worked out how you thought it would. Maybe a supplier has just pulled out of a deal at the last minute or a company restructure has thrown a spanner in the works. Maybe you're stuck and haven't figured out the next step or maybe it's completely dead but still on your radar: abandoned but still on the road; done but not quite dusted. What's been hanging around for way too long, gathering dust on your to-do list?

When we have too many things on red, we feel frustrated. Nothing is moving forward, everything is stuck: we need to figure out a way forward. When we have a few things on red – but stuck permanently there – it might be tempting to ignore them, and let the green traffic work its way around them. But that still takes up space on the road and makes it harder work for the traffic to flow.

What do you need to release? To take off the road completely?

What do you need to take action on, to get unstuck?

What do you need help with?

AMBER: WHAT'S ON HOLD?

What is pending on your to-do list? What are you waiting on someone else for? What will you get round to someday? That piece of information you're waiting on, the lead time you need to give someone else to make a decision, the time it takes for an order to be processed or a decision to be authorised, the work you've delegated, decisions you're delaying…

Whether you've chosen to put that piece of work on pending or you're waiting for someone else to come back to you, revving your engines at an amber light, poised to take action but not actually going anywhere, takes effort and energy and distracts you from the work that you can be getting on with.

What do you need to park instead?

@waiting: for the things you are waiting on
Waiting for Joe from accounts to send you those figures before you can do anything else with your presentation? Tracking a missing parcel and need to wait seven days before you can chase it? Want to set yourself a reminder to follow up a sales enquiry if you haven't heard back within the next two weeks?

Keep this separate from your actions, the things that you can be working on right now, so that you don't create a stop–start momentum where you keep bouncing between 'Yes, I can do that: go go go' and 'No, I can't do that right now, still waiting: stand down'.

But do keep track of it because then you won't need to carry it around in your head any more. I keep it in a separate @waiting category of my to-do list, away from my actions, together in one place where I can check in regularly and nudge or chase as need be.

TIP

Instead of having a giant to-do list, I separate my tasks into categories and assign an @ tag to make it easy to find. So, when I want to find all the things I'm waiting for, I search for @waiting. If I want to find all the things that I need to talk to my husband about, I search for @grante.

Ideas park: for the things you choose to put off

Is it just me or do our best ideas come when we are trying to focus on something else? An idea for a blog post, an interesting new tool you've discovered, campaigns you might want to run in future, a project that's on the back burner, a book to add to the reading list, that brilliant shiny new idea you've just had when you were trying to focus on something else.

That's when an ideas park comes in handy. This is somewhere to physically store your ideas, out of your head, so they stop distracting you and are kept safe for you to come back to when you are ready to actually do something with them. You could use a separate notebook, the back pages of your notebook, a physical or electronic file, a tag or category on your to-do list app or, as one of my clients did, keep an actual ideas jar on your desk: every time she has an idea that is different from what she is focusing on, she writes it down on a piece of paper, folds it up and puts it in the jar. That way she gets it out of her head and keeps it safe – her ideas jar becomes like a treasure chest, full of ideas to explore when she is ready.

GREEN: WHAT'S GOOD TO GO?

So, everything should be green, right? Well, not quite. Giving everything the green light creates exactly the kind of chaos you would imagine if all the traffic lights at a busy junction suddenly turned green. You have havoc: cars cutting up left, right and centre, some spectacular crashes and near misses, lots of swerving and, eventually, gridlock... it would be total chaos.

We can do anything, but not everything at once – so the saying goes. Our productivity depends on how well we manage the traffic as much as how well we drive the car (do the work). And, when we manage it well, the traffic flows and driving becomes a dream, rather than a danger.

Incoming!

How do you manage the incoming stuff? Do you just tend to react to whoever's shouting the loudest or to what happens to land in your inbox when you're looking? Do you deal with things as soon as they arrive or do you let it all pile up and see which one floats to the top? Do you catch everything that arrives or do some things fall through the cracks? Or do you duck and hide and hope nothing sticks?

If there's always more work to be done (and, arguably, more work than can be done), dealing directly with the incoming is exhausting, unrewarding and can lead to perpetual firefighting and constantly reacting to whatever's shouting the loudest, rather than progressing the things that matter to you and that perhaps nobody else would chase you for. But, not dealing with the incoming can also lead to being bogged down by backlogs, missing things, forgetting things and a constant sense of playing catch up and not quite knowing what you've overlooked, that might come back to bite you.

As a Productivity Ninja, I teach people the CORD Productivity Model to help them manage everything they need to get done in work (and life).[4]

CORD stands for capture and collect, organise, review and do.

1. CAPTURE AND COLLECT

The first stage, capture and collect, is simply about having a robust method of capturing all the incoming stuff that you want to keep in some way, shape or form. It might be one for the ideas park or an action that needs doing this week. At the point where it's incoming, you probably don't know yet. But, if it has passed the first stage of 'do I want to pay it some attention?', then you need a way to capture it, rather than storing it in your head.

2. ORGANISE

This stage is about defining the work. The job here is to filter from a mass of ideas to 'what's worth doing?' and 'what's the next action?'. This part of traffic control is about parking what's pending or waiting, deleting what's not worth doing and making sure what goes on the road is fit for purpose – that is, well-defined, specific next actions.

3. REVIEW

Review is where we go fully into boss mode. Check in with the bigger picture. How is everything going? What's on track? What's next? This is where we make decisions about direction and priority. What do we need to make space for this week? What's our focus? It's also where we check in with ourselves: how am I feeling?; what am I resisting?; how's my energy?; am I making time for what's important to me? and what do I need to do differently?

4. DO

Do is about ruthless execution and effortless momentum. Having captured, defined and reviewed the work, this is where we get down and 'do'. Drive the car. Focus on the road ahead. Make the journey. Get the job done. Even then, there are things that can get in the way – distractions, obstacles, bumps in the road, unexpected road closures and U-turns. Things we need to respond and react to in the moment but, with less of the reactive in our day to day, we find we are more prepped and primed to respond in the moment.

5. Done

Technically, this is part of the 'do' stage – or the result of the do stage of the CORD Productivity Model – but it's something that so often gets overlooked, I think it's worth a mention here.

Done. Actually ticking it off the list, closing it off and celebrating that achievement before moving on.

We often miss out on this stage because we're so busy moving on to the next one, but here's why it's important: it's about switching off. It's about actually finishing – doing that very last step that marks the project complete, instead of letting it hang around as that tiny thing you just have to do.

For me, this is where I'm tempted to keep tweaking, instead of publishing and sending it out there. To keep editing, keep working on it. For my husband, this is the point where he stops slightly short of the finish line. He's put in all the effort and got the project almost there, then leaves the very last thing undone: the edging on the living room floor; the fairy lights and mirror that add that final touch to our daughter's room, still sitting in its packaging. Whether you keep working at it or you stop just short of being able to declare the task complete, either way, you keep it in motion. It's still part of the traffic you are managing, still taking up space on the road, still requiring a little bit of your attention.

Maybe that last thing is actually just filing the file away, deleting the email or archiving the project, instead of leaving it lying around like an abandoned car on the road. There is nothing left to be done but it's still taking up space and you're still having to navigate around it.

In place vs. in use

Kitchen designers and professional organisers both work on the principle of dynamic order, the idea that things do not stay in one place all the time, but everything needs a place to be 'in use' and to be 'in place' when it's not in use. For example, when my children are playing, the toys are in use and belong on the floor. It can look like a mess, but the toys are exactly where they're supposed to be. When they have finished playing, that's when the toys need to be tidied away and to go back in place.

Clutter happens when we leave things in use, instead of putting them back in place: the letters we read but don't action; the paperwork we leave on the worktop because we still need to do something with it; tasks and projects we have on the go that we haven't mentally put down; things we don't need any more but haven't let go of. Things we do need but haven't quite decided where they go. That's when we end up tripping over toys, when things get broken and my children look at a sea of toys and declare they don't have anything to play with. Eventually, they abandon the whole mess and find another space to invade/play in.

I see the same thing happen with emails in the 'Getting Your Inbox to Zero' workshops I run. Inboxes start as a place for incoming items then, typically, become a dumping ground for emails that:

- need to be actioned

- don't need to be actioned

- need to be read

- have been read but still need figuring out

- are waiting on someone else's action

- are waiting on your decision

- have been actioned (but not quite filed away).

Do you have too many things in use?

When we have too many things in use, we don't use any of them properly. Everything gets in the way and nothing gets enough focus. We just end up paper shuffling, wading through the mess and yelping when we stand on LEGO. We move things around rather than use them. We find ourselves surrounded by toys rather than playing with them, surrounded by work rather than actually doing the work.

Putting things back in place – whether that is a physical place or mentally switching off – can help us to focus on the things that do need our attention: the actions, the work, the things we need to do.

It's also about momentum and motivation; the satisfaction of getting things done. When we stop to acknowledge our progress, it gives us fuel to do more. It reminds us of what we are capable of.

> **TIP**
>
> How often do you stop to celebrate your progress? Try writing a ta-da! list at the end of a day, week or month to celebrate your achievements instead of just focusing on your to-do list.

Clarity in where you work: noise control

With open offices and open communication channels on the go 24/7, it's easy to find yourself being continually interrupted and distracted. A study of Microsoft workers found that, when working on something that required a significant level of focus, it took an average of 15 minutes to recover attention from a 1-minute interruption.

One minute to take that call, check that email, answer that colleague's question; fifteen minutes to recover your attention, remember where you were up to, reread the last paragraph, get back into the flow of what you were doing before.

Ever get to the end of the day, when you're closing down your computer, and you find that email you started to write at 9 am? Recent research from Middle Tennessee State University also found that being distracted by personal social media leads to negative effects on efficiency and well-being. Participants were asked to watch a 15-minute video on a computer, with tabs left open for a number of social media sites, including Facebook, Twitter and LinkedIn. They were monitored to see how often they checked social media and were tested on the video's content. Those who used the sites more did not perform as well as those who used them less – and were also found to have 'higher levels of technostress and lower happiness'.

How many times do you get interrupted in your working day? How often are you distracted by what else is going on in your world, in your head or on your desktop? How much of your attention is that stealing?

Common culprits for distraction (as reported by workshop delegates) include:

- colleagues in the office
- phone calls
- emails
- your boss
- instant messaging chat
- social media
- the report that's still sitting on your desk from last week
- background noise
- me! thoughts of other work, nags, reminders, new ideas, etc.

What about sensory noise?

Our senses gather some 11 million bits per second from our environment – but our conscious mind can process only about 50 bits per second. We all filter out information, but some people are more sensitive to certain noise than others.

My husband, for example, works best in total silence. He is particularly sensitive to noise that comes from people – chatter and crowds. Blocking out background noise takes up a certain amount of effort and energy so, even when he can filter out the noise, he doesn't give his full attention to the work at hand. He notices that noise also creeps up on him. He may not notice it building up until, all of a sudden, it's completely unbearable.

In contrast, I don't work too well in a totally quiet or static environment. I find that background noise and movement stimulates me and gets my brain working better than in complete silence. The only exception is when I'm on a phone call or a webinar – when what I need to focus on is auditory. Otherwise, give me the humdrum of a café, with people coming and going, background chatter and music I can hum to, any day. In fact, that is where most of this book has been written – in the corner of a wonderful little local café that serves amazing aubergine caponata.

What's your optimal working environment? And how well is your current environment working for you? Does it stimulate you, overstimulate you or bore you? Does it get your creative juices flowing or overload your senses? Does it wake up your brain or shut it down?

If you find your environment is too much on the noisy side (or has the wrong kind of noise), here are some ways you can turn it down.

REDUCE DIGITAL NOISE

- Turn off email notifications.

- Turn off social media notifications.

- Unsubscribe from newsletters or notifications you no longer need.

- Set up a rule to filter out the things you want to pay less attention to and move them into a 'circulars' or 'read later' folder.

- Put chat programs to offline/unavailable for the times when you don't want to talk.

- Turn off automatic send/receive (or go into work offline mode on your email).

- Turn off the Wi-Fi.

- Don't leave email open in the background (the same goes for social media).

- Close tabs/windows when you've finished before moving on to the next thing.

REDUCE PHYSICAL NOISE

- Use headphones.
- Close the door.
- Change location: work from home/meeting room/café.
- Have an agreed 'do not disturb' signal in open offices.
- Communicate your availability (more on this in Chapter 6).
- Clear clutter from your desk.

REDUCE NOISE IN YOUR OWN HEAD

- Write it down, get it out of your head.
- Use a trusted second-brain system to capture ideas, reminders and nags.
- Focus on one thing at a time (more on multitasking in Chapter 10).
- Give yourself a visual reminder of the thing you're working on (e.g. Post-it Note).
- Calm your mind monkeys (more on this in Chapter 3).

Clarity in the chaos beyond your control

Responsibility vs. response-ability

'The day-to-day stuff I feel like I have some control over – to a degree. What really gets me is when some-thing gets taken out of my hands, but I'm left to deal with the fall out. I'm still responsible but I'm not in control, and I convince myself chaos reigns.'

What does it really mean to be responsible? Perhaps it's more helpful to think about it as response-able. To take responsibility is to choose how you respond. In situations where we may not be able to take control of what's going on around us, the thing we can control is our response. We can choose how we respond.

We can choose not to take responsibility for what someone else has done but, instead, take responsibility over how we respond, in our emotions, our thoughts and our actions.

We can choose to focus on the frustration, the anger, the feeling of being overwhelmed. We can beat ourselves up with guilt for not, somehow, being able to make this problem go away or avoid it in the first place. We choose to try and control the uncontrollable – and, effectively, choose to feed the chaos. Or we can choose to focus on what we can do rather than what we can't, to look to 'what now?' instead of dwell on 'what happened?' and ask ourselves 'what can I do?' rather than 'why me?'.

When we choose to let go of being the victim, 'why has this happened to me?', or the perpetrator, 'this is all my fault, if only I...', that's when we can take control, over our own actions and our own response. We can let go of the drama, the guilt, the fear, the anger and the frustration – and see the situation in a new light: a problem, yes, but not a personal attack; a setback, yes, but not insurmountable; a tricky position, perhaps, but not trapped; a curveball, not the end of the world; a plot twist and you're still holding the pen.

That's when the chaos stops being our chaos and we no longer need to control it. We just need to navigate and plot a course that works best for us.

> 'You really have to evolve into a [mindset] where you're only going to hold yourself accountable for the things you can control. If you bear every burden of the world, you're going to die a young death as a CEO.
>
> 'If you're going to say, "Oh my god, what am I going to do about the French economy? It's so terrible right now" – you can't do a damn thing about that and you can't worry about that. You just have to hold yourself accountable for those things you personally can have an impact on and leave the rest behind.'
>
> **JEFF IMMELT, CHIEF EXECUTIVE OF GENERAL ELECTRIC[5]**

Expect the unexpected

How much does your schedule depend on everything running like clockwork? How prepared are you for the unexpected? How much margin do you have for mistakes? I'm a recovering perfectionist. I've always set myself high standards, but I've never demanded perfection from others. In fact, even when I've been hard on myself, I've still been encouraging others to be kinder to themselves. I'm too nice to be a perfectionist when it comes to other people, or so I thought.

It was midnight. I was home after a two-hour drive and I had a workshop the next morning. I should have been sleeping but, instead, I found myself printing. I thought I had it all worked out: I knew it was going to be a bit of a three-day marathon, I had scoped ahead, taken a deep breath and got everything prepared and lined up in advance. For once, I was not the one leaving it to the last minute. This time it was someone else – someone else's mistake and oversight that I had to sacrifice sleep to rectify. Disaster was averted and, even though I had a terrible night's sleep, the workshop went brilliantly.

But it did get me thinking: yes, it was someone else's mistake, yes they should have spotted it, yes they could have given themselves more time (it had also been a busy season for them). No, it was not my job to make sure they did theirs and, yes, we would be having a conversation about it. (Thankfully, I knew better than to fire off an email when tired and very grumpy!)

I realised this: when my schedule is so tight that there is no margin for error, then, by default, I am demanding perfection – not just from me – but from everyone around me.

Because I simply have no time to accommodate mistakes. No time for the waiter who has got my order wrong. No time for the learner driver who is stalled at the roundabout. No time for the cashier who is trying to get to grips with the till on their first day or the apprentice who is completely lost trying to navigate the corporate culture. No time for my children to have a meltdown at the door. No time for my colleague to notice, let alone recover, from their mistake.

And it's not just to do with mistakes. A friend of mine tweeted the other day that his son had chosen to wake him at 5 am on 'Daddy Monday'.

I could completely relate – as my daughter went through a phase where any wake-up time that started with a 6 was joyously celebrated. But it made me smile that he saw Daddy Monday as a day when he didn't need to get up early, because he was at home with his son and not at work. Another way to look at it would be: 'Daddy Monday is precisely the day when I need to get up early – and I don't even need to set an alarm to do so.'

If we work in a last-minute environment, for a company going through rapid change or do anything involving children or animals, part of our job is dealing with the predictably unpredictable. Change is part of the territory. And, when we have the scope and capacity to deal with it, we are actually pretty good at responding to change. There have been many occasions where I have been more than happy to bail a client out of a last-minute crisis, calmly talked my son through tying the laces on the shoes he insisted on wearing or saved dinner by thinking creatively.

It's when I'm already running late and my son decides it **has** to be those shoes, when I'm rushing to meet a deadline and the hot potato hits my inbox, or when I'm at the end of my tether and I spill the spaghetti down the sink, that's when it becomes chaos.

It's chaos only when we feel out of control but when we are prepared, equipped with some spare capacity and expect the unexpected, we find we can roll with the punches, dance with the change and respond with remarkable agility and grace.

Dealing with uncertainty

I have a theory about the creative process. We start with a brilliant idea. It might be the best thing since sliced bread, it might be a quirky little idea that just might have legs. Whatever it is, it shines enough to spark our interest, for us to decide it's worth pursuing. By the end of the creative process, we will have created something. It might be nothing like we envisioned initially – or it might be exactly what we had in mind – but it's something beautiful, whole and real. What happens in between is a vast, empty, wild land of unchartered territory. There is nothing here but the potential for everything, a blank canvas, waiting for you to fill with words, colour, models, formulae – whatever your medium might be. Whatever you can imagine, you can create.

Welcome to the void. The void can be a playground or an assault course, a sanctuary or a prison. It all depends on what we bring in. Here's what you need to know about the void:

YOU WILL NOT KNOW EVERYTHING

So stop trying. Let go of having to have all the pieces of the jigsaw in place before you start. As Martin Luther King Jr said, 'You do not have to see the whole staircase, just take the first step.' The journey is created as you take it and some of the best stories only come together, where everything makes sense, at the end.

THERE IS NO RIGHT

The more we obsess about having to get it right, the more confused we'll become. In unchartered territory, right has not been invented yet. All there is is possibility, and right is whichever you choose. Instead of 'I have to get it right', try telling yourself 'I get to make this up as I go along.' Embrace the opportunity to shape the outcome as you go along (rather than trying to find the outcome).

YOU HAVE THE RIGHT TO CHANGE YOUR MIND

It's about exploration, not expectation. Focus on discovery, which means you will probably find dead ends and dodgy alleyways as well as wide open spaces. If you chase a rabbit down a hole and find yourself somewhere you don't want to be, you can always find a different route. Each step you take is meaningful, but not set in stone.

WHATEVER YOU IMAGINE, YOU CREATE

In the absence of knowing, we fill the void with our imagination. What are you imagining? Are you imagining all the things that could go wrong, all the what-if disaster scenarios? Are you focusing on how much you don't know, rather than what you do know? Are you internalising the uncertainty? Not just dealing with the unknown, but focusing on how much **you** don't know, turning doubt into self-doubt. If that is what we fill the void with, that is precisely what we will create: more uncertainty, more fear, more doubt, more worry, chaos and confusion.

Instead, focus on what you do know. Remind yourself of all the truths of what you can do, what you do know, what you are capable of and what you are equipped with. Focus on what you can see – and imagine what's possible from there. Reframe your thoughts from 'I don't know' to 'This I know... and this is what I'm discovering/working on/figuring out.'

YOU WILL GET TIRED

Making decisions is hard work. Even on the days when it feels like you haven't done anything, made any progress or have anything to show for it (perhaps especially those days), the chances are you have been doing a lot of mental heavy lifting.

Research into decision fatigue suggests that our ability to make decisions is like a muscle. Yes, you can gradually build it up to be stronger and more resilient but, at the end of the day, it always gets tired. In fact, every decision you make is like another rep in a workout. That's why parole board judges are more likely to give favourable rulings at the beginning of the day or after a lunch break. As the day goes on, decision fatigue sets in and they are more likely to settle for the default answer: no.[6]

I have noticed decision fatigue in the process of writing this book, especially at the beginning, when everything is possible, but undefined. Surrounded by uncertainty, with so many decisions to make, I found myself going stir crazy if someone gave me yet another decision to make: 'What do you mean you can't find any socks?'.

Sometimes, I didn't even notice that I was carrying decisions around in my head, mulling them over on the walk to school, until 'what's for tea mummy?' made me feel as if someone had just pulled me away from a high-wire trapeze act and dumped me in the middle of a rugby game.

The more decisions we have to make, the harder each one will become and the more likely we will be to default to the easiest decision – whether that's to grab the nearest bar of chocolate, crash on the sofa, walk away from that important-but-tricky conversation, explode in a fit of road rage or say yes to that extra piece of responsibility you haven't quite figured out how to extricate yourself from.

And the more we'll crave certainty as well. I don't think it's an accident that, when we are prone to procrastination, all sorts of mundane things like sorting the pen drawer, watering the plants or doing the ironing become incredibly attractive. It's the certainty we crave: where we know exactly what we need to do, rather than having to figure something out.

We can't change the void, or avoid the void. It's part of the process, part of the journey we need to press through, to get to the other side. But here are some things that will help to bring clarity to the void:

Give yourself a break. If you are in a season of high uncertainty, honour the fact that your brain is doing some pretty taxing work and make some concessions. Let someone else choose what you have for dinner; work out what you're wearing at the beginning of the week. Let go of the unimportant decisions: so what if the children want to change into their pyjamas at 4 pm on a Sunday afternoon? Does it really matter which shade of blue you go for? And do you really need to buy something from duty free? Excuse yourself from a meeting and tell your team you trust them to make the decisions. Pace yourself: limit the amount of high decision-making projects you have on the go. Maybe wait until you've finished the book before you start redecorating the bedroom.

Ask for help. Sometimes the simplest of decisions can appear impossible when we are suffering from decision fatigue. So, if you know you are dealing with some mental heavy lifting, ask other people for their perspective and, where possible, delegate your decisions. Set up support structures so that you have colleagues you can talk things through with before you have to present an idea to senior stakeholders. I called my boss the other day to ask his decision on something that, normally, I could have figured out for myself. 'I'm suffering from decision fatigue,' I told him. 'What do I need to do here?' In about three minutes, he had worked it out and saved me hours of deliberating. We all have times when we are overloaded with decision fatigue. Whether that's because of a big creative project or a high season of change and unpredictability, the more we can recognise that in ourselves and each other, the more we can help and ask for help.

Ask good questions. Questions such as 'What do I do?', 'What if...', 'What about...' and 'Is this any good?' tend to send us round in circles. However, questions such as 'What's the next step?', 'What do I know already?', 'What do I need to move forward?' 'Who could I ask?' and 'What would make this irresistible?' are more likely to give us answers we can use.

Lower the stakes. We all want to do our jobs well, to get things right (whether you feel like you're doing your life's work or just something to tide you over and keep a roof over your head). The fact that we care is what gives birth to our best work, but the pressure can also feed our performance anxiety. If looking at your deadline or your word count freaks you out, stop looking! Focus on whatever will give you enough motivation to keep going – the next 100 words, the next 20 minutes, the next conversation, the next meal you make, the next person you encourage, the next mile you run, the next staircase you walk, the next step you take...

Make it fun. When you forget about the crazy deadline or the high-stakes pressure and lose yourself in the process of creating, the void can actually be a pretty fun place. We can lose ourselves in the flow when we are unrestricted by expectation, free to charter new territory and make it up as we go along. The trick I have found is to time myself at the gate. Set the time when I arrive and the time when I have to pack up and leave the playground. Everything I do in between is free-flow: no expectations, no targets, just write. And trust – a heap load of trust – that what comes out at the other end will be something beautiful, whole and real.

Over to you

What's my territory? Where am I choosing to spend my time and focus?

Work:..

Worry:..

How's my traffic control? What three things can I do to get things flowing better?

1. ....

2. ....

3. ....

How do I deal with the incoming? Which stage of the CORD Productivity Model do I need to work on?

....

What do I currently have in use that needs to be put in place?

....

My optimal working environment

Three changes I can make to reduce the noise:

1. ....

2. ....

3. ....

One thing I can do to improve my response-ability:

....

Where I need to give myself more space and capacity to expect the unexpected:

....

Where's my void? What do I choose to fill it with?

....

Chapter 3

Mind monkeys and lizard brain

Why do we leave things to the last minute – and then freak out at the deadline? Why, when we need courage, do we scare ourselves more? Why do we insist on winding ourselves up with disaster thinking? Why do we say we want one thing, then do the complete opposite?

The answer is this: we have monkeys living in our brain.

In his book *The Chimp Paradox*, Professor Steve Peters describes the brain as having three different parts:

- **The human brain**: which makes logical, purposeful decisions, motivated by fulfilment, self-development, morals and ethics.

- **The chimp brain**: which is responsible for survival, driven by primitive emotional drivers, such as fear, ego and rage (and, yes, the reproductive drive). It is extremely risk averse and sees all change as potential danger. It will protect you from being in the limelight, being visible, bucking the trend, doing something new, taking risks, making changes – because what it doesn't know it can't control and what it can't control it can't stop from hurting you.

- **The computer brain**: automatic habits that can be operated by the human or the chimp.

Author, high-profile blogger and entrepreneur Seth Godin refers to the chimp brain as the lizard brain:

> 'Want to know why so many companies can't keep up with Apple? It's because they compromise, have meetings, work to fit in, fear the critics and generally work to appease the lizard... The amygdala isn't going away. Your lizard brain is here to stay, and your job is to figure out how to quiet it and ignore it.'

I call it my mind monkeys – I'm not sure if there are many or if there is one. Sometimes it's just one, sometimes it feels like there's a whole gang of them chattering away in there! Whether you see it as your mind monkey, your lizard brain or your inner critic, there is definitely something that goes on inside our heads, that creates resistance, generates fear, tempts us to procrastinate and drives us to distraction.

What's going on in your head? And what can you do about it? Let's take a deeper look, shall we?

Monkey tactics: six things your monkey will do

1. Distract you

*'Hey! Come and play! You **have** to see this! Ooh, shiny...'*

Your monkey gets bored easily. It likes to play. Faced with the spreadsheet that bores the pants off you, your monkey sees it as his mission to find you something much more interesting to do. Faced with a big problem to solve, something difficult or scary, your monkey finds a million things that would take your mind off it.

Essentially, your monkey just wants everyone to get along and have fun. So, when it sees you struggling with something, it helpfully offers you some light relief. Except your monkey is also extremely short-sighted. It has the attention span of a three-year-old. It can't see that the struggle will only get worse if you keep leaving it or that, eventually, you'll have to hand in that piece of work anyway and feel awful about the poor job you did, or that beyond the struggle is a whole heap of fun, if you can just get this boring bit done first...

All it sees is the bad and the boring and offers you something shiny and sparkly to brighten up your day: checking your emails, playing that game, meeting someone for coffee, changing the fonts on your website, watering the plants, catching up with Carol about her weekend, fixing the zip on your bag, updating your phone, looking into that insurance deal, sorting out your sock drawer. Distraction monkey makes everything seem compelling.

Bloggers Tim Urban and Andrew Finn call this the Instant Gratification Monkey who just wants to go and play in the Dark Playground – the place where you get a fleeting hit of light relief and feel dreadful afterwards.[1] The trick is to tempt the monkey into the dark woods (where the hard work happens) without leaving, and far enough down the track that the happy playground (job done, reward) comes into view.

2. Beat you up

'Seriously, who do you think you are? You can't do this!'

Remember how excited you were when you first had that idea? Or the motivation you had when you bounced out of that conference? Or even the last award you won when you **knew** that it was all worthwhile, that finally here was proof that you **can** do it?

This heavy-hitting monkey still comes back with the same message: you're not good enough/clever enough/fast enough/big enough/academic enough/business-savvy enough/assertive enough/charismatic enough/disciplined enough/creative enough... or as good as your friend/colleague/predecessor/competitor...

It's not very creative, but it is strong. Self-doubt and comparison are its main punches – predictable, but very powerful. It doesn't have to justify itself because, as long as it makes you feel small, it will appear big and be in charge.

The weird thing is, this monkey's sole aim is actually to protect you. It thinks there is a bigger danger beyond that door, so it casts itself as the bouncer, whose sole aim is to stop you from making a fool of yourself. It figures that it's better to put you down than to let someone else do it. That it's safer to stop you from taking that risk than for you to fall into danger.

3. Put you off

*'This is a **bad** idea! Back away. Don't even go there. It's all going to go horribly wrong. What do you think you're **doing**? Really?! What will people think?'*

Combined with convincing you that you don't have what it takes, your monkey might also take a second line of attack to convince you that the quest you are considering is far too dangerous, impossible and completely not worth it.

It's too hard. It won't work. We tried it before, remember? Don't bother. Save yourself the headache and the heartache, love. Maybe another time, but not right now, hey? You don't have anything to prove. Give yourself a break.

4. Weigh you down

> *'You can't do that! What will people think? Besides, you haven't got time for that. Look at all this stuff you've got to do, and all the people who rely on you. You can't let them down.'*

Your monkey might also try and remind you of all your other obligations: things you have already committed to, people who are relying on you, things you should be doing.

Especially, when you're working on something that matters to you, that perhaps no one else is going to chase you up on, your monkey may weigh you down with more serious responsibility and try and put you off taking on that dream project that you would really love to do.

5. Wear you down

> *'But what if... what about... have you thought about this?'*

'Ok,' your monkey is thinking, 'if you're going to pursue this, you'd better be armed with **all** the available information. Let's start with all the things that could go wrong. All the variables you have to get right. You call it disaster thinking, I call it being realistic and prepared.'

You might not be put off entirely, but it sure takes a lot of energy to answer your monkey's questions. Remember decision fatigue? Every question you answer is another decision you have to make, another level of good judgement depleted. By the time you have finished going round in circles, you've forgotten what you were doing, you notice it's nearly 5 o'clock and you call it a day.

6. Fill your head with chatter

'Nope! Hey, look! Did you know? That's so dumb. Who would seriously... Oh, look at that... Lalalalalalalala.'

If the bullying and scare tactics don't work, your monkey might just throw a tantrum instead and fill your head with a whole load of chatter. It might throw you a combination of put downs and put offs, some what ifs and what abouts, but all you can hear is a whole lot of noise.

Your monkey is just shouting, you don't have a clue what it's saying. It's loud and you can't think straight. Your brain simply freezes, gives up trying to do any amount of sensible thinking and goes on strike.

Dealing with your monkey

Do not fight the monkey.

Listen, the monkey is strong. You can't overpower it and it is stubborn. It won't go away if you shout at it. In fact, the monkey loves shouting matches. It will happily shout back and keep shouting back. Fighting the monkey is exhausting and doesn't work very well. Ignoring the monkey is also tricky. You can try and ignore it for a while but, when it keeps following you around, tapping you on the shoulder, eventually that becomes torture.

What can you do instead? Here are some tactics to handle your mind monkeys.

Distract your monkey

I'm sitting in a café right now, writing this book. The irony has not escaped me that I have just spent the best part of the last three weeks trying to beat my mind monkeys off with a stick. But, right now, my mind monkeys are happy. They're quietly tapping and swaying away to the music in the background. They have been fed good food, tea and coffee. The change of scenery and the lack of complete silence have, in a funny way, quietened the noise in my head and the words are starting to flow again.

Could a change of scenery to the canteen, a meeting room or a different office distract your mind monkeys?

Invite your monkey to play

Monkeys love games. So, why not turn your work into a game? Have a tax return or expenses to complete? Buddy up with an accountability partner and turn it into a competition. Hate confrontation, but love puzzles? Turn it into a puzzle that you're trying to solve. Earn the reward of doing something fun every time you do something difficult.

THE POMODORO TECHNIQUE

When you have a whole day's work ahead of you, or a stack of work to get through, the thought of slogging through can be demotivating. The idea behind Francesco Cirillo's Pomodoro Technique is to work in dashes, to alternate 25 minutes of focus with a 5-minute procrastination break.[2]

Take that big piece of work you keep putting off: why not just start with a 25-minute stint, then give yourself full permission to move onto something else? Or what about the backlog of filing that is piling up? Set your timer and see how much you can get through in 25 minutes (or 10 minutes, if that feels more manageable – feel free to make up your own rules here!). Give yourself a time limit for the piece of editing you know you could spend days on if you could get away with it, and see how much you can get done in that time.

EAT THAT FROG![3]

That thing you keep putting off – the one you would really rather not do – that's hanging round like a bad smell, that's your frog. The frog follows you around every day, making you feel bad, but not quite bad enough to actually do it. Every time you look at it, your heart sinks. You pause and wonder how to tackle it, then move onto something a lot more doable. Every time you tick something else off the list, that sense of satisfaction is dampened by the fact that your frog is still there, taunting you and mocking you.

The idea is simple. If you eat a smelly, slimy frog for breakfast, everything you have afterwards will taste sweet. The game is to take one thing you have been putting off – one frog – and commit to tackling it first thing in the morning, before you do anything else. Before you get too tired, before you get distracted or waylaid, before checking your emails, grabbing a coffee or starting to chat to colleagues. Before something else crops up, just get your head down for, say, 30 minutes and get it done. Before your monkey wakes up and starts shouting at you. Just do it.

The effect is brilliant. Not only has the frog gone and is no longer able to haunt you (and probably didn't taste anywhere near as bad as you thought it would), but the boost to your motivation and self-esteem makes your monkey feel brilliant, too.

'Look at me! I've just eaten a frog! Ra! If I can do that, I can take on the world! What's next? Come on, what's next on that to-do list? Let's do this thing – woohoo!'

Who's afraid of the big bad phone?

I want to tell you about one of my clients: let's call her Tina. I'm so proud of her.

Tina was afraid of the phone. Not cowering, gibbering-wreck afraid – no way – but dreading, feet-dragging, easily distracted, I will-do-anything-to-avoid-it afraid. Ever get that? Yup, me too. But Tina had had enough. Fear was standing between her and her clients: the people who need her help, the people she loves working with. She decided she could no longer tolerate that fear. So, what did Tina do? She decided to stare fear in the face.

She set herself a target: to make five calls each day and to start logging her fear factor:

- before making calls: 8/10, 6/10, 7/10...

- and afterwards: 4/10, 3/10, 2/10...

What she noticed was this: 'Actually, the fear just before doing something feels much worse than actually doing it. I feel much better once I get off the phone, having made a call, than I do just before I make the call.'

Fear was the enemy, not the phone. Making phone calls actually made her feel better. That's the thing about fear. Fear fuels resistance and steals enjoyment, contentment and satisfaction. Fear is the thing that has us saying:

'I know it's just... but I just can't seem to bring myself to do it.'

'I know I can, but I'm doing everything else to avoid it.'

'I know it's silly, but... anyway, I haven't got time now.'

Fear is a shadow. When it lurks behind you or looms over you, its presence is big, bad and scary. But a shadow has no substance. When you shine a light at it, face it head on, its power disperses.

What about you? Where is fear holding you back? What would you discover if you faced it head on?

Just add fun

In the world of business and productivity, things can get a little too serious for my liking. And, when things get serious, fear, overwhelm and procrastination come out to play.

Fun, on the other hand, is naturally motivating. It comes easily, it doesn't overwhelm and we don't need to psyche ourselves up for it. Fun engages our creativity and brings out our best ideas. It's easy to stay focused when you're having fun. You don't have to try. It just has you engaged. Distractions become less distracting. Procrastination less appealing. Fun is sustainable. It's easy to keep going when you're having fun.

What would make it fun? Here are some ideas to get you started:

- Pair up and race a colleague to get your inbox to zero/expenses submitted/tax return done.

- Put on some music and dance, if you want to.

- Talk through that article instead of writing it – and get it transcribed, if you really don't want to write it.

- Set a stop watch and see how quickly you can get something done.

- Use a timer to see how much you can get done in the next 10 minutes.

- Add colour: change the colour of your spreadsheet, get the highlighters and Post-it Notes out.

- Get crafty and physically make something for your next presentation.

- Change the environment: stand up or sit on the floor, go to a different room, escape outdoors, visit the art gallery, a café or the park.

- Start your breakfast meeting with hot bacon rolls – an added bonus to ensure everyone turns up on time.

- Run a photo competition instead of your regular team updates – one photo that summarises your biggest highlight – maybe with a caption competition.

- Move your meeting – literally. Go for a walking meeting: round the block for a quick update, into the forest for some deep discussions or down by the beach (if you are lucky enough to live by the sea).

Add your own here ....

- ....

- ....

What would make it irresistible?

This question comes from my friend Jennie Harland-Khan, who runs her business around the concept of Irresistible Living: 'What would be an irresistible way of doing this?'[4]

Instead of fighting that resistance, making yourself do something you think you **should**, what could you change about the job at hand – or how you do it – that would make it irresistible?

This question led Jennie to create her Irresistible Roadshow – overcoming her resistance to running webinars by hosting Google Hangouts from five different locations in two months: Morocco, Lanzarote, Chamonix, LA and Perth. How is that for irresistibility, huh? As a total travel fanatic, this solution was perfect for Jennie. She has shaped her own life and business around travelling and she had reason to be in all those places anyway, so it wasn't a pipe dream. Suddenly, something that she knew she **should** do became something she couldn't wait to do.

Irresistibility overrides resistance. It might still be hard work or scary stuff but, when you turn up the irresistibility, that stuff stops stopping you. You power through the tough parts, put up with the mundane and find ways around the challenges because, quite frankly, you can't wait to do it.

What would make your something irresistible for you?

Devising your own game

Games get a bad press for distracting us from being productive, but understanding how games work can also help us to come up with some creative and compelling ways of getting our work done. Head of Games

Design and Production at Totem Learning, Helen Routledge, suggests that there are three golden rules of game design that apply to productivity:[5]

1. Save the world, one step at a time.

2. Don't forget the rewards.

3. Name your distractions as the bad guys.

1. SAVE THE WORLD, ONE STEP AT A TIME

'Games are nested problems. They give you an overarching problem to solve, say save the world, defeat the bad guy, build a city, but they don't tell you how to get there. They give you a long-term goal and it is up to the player themselves to work out how to get there. Also a game doesn't just throw you in and say "hey dude, go and save the world", and then leave you to it. What actually happens is that you save the world through very incremental tasks that individually may not seem so important but that actually come together to have a great impact. These are short-term goals.'

If you find yourself freaking out at a big goal, don't be put off if you can't see the whole path. Often the journey becomes clearer only when we start taking steps. Focus on the small steps that take you closer, instead of trying to save the world in one fell swoop.

2. DON'T FORGET THE REWARDS

'Games always reward a player for doing something that moves them closer to the ultimate goal, whether it's Experience Points (XP), new equipment, stars, coins or even just points, you always receive something for the effort you put in.'

One of my colleagues gives himself a gold star for every Pomodoro he achieves. In his book *How to be a Knowledge Ninja*, Graham Allcott suggests earning 'fun points' for every unit of study or work, then trading in those fun points for guilt-free pleasure: 1 point for an hour of watching Netflix, 2 points for coffee with a friend, 9 points for a whole day off to spend as you please.

3. NAME YOUR DISTRACTIONS AS THE BAD GUYS

'Give them names and think about their powers. By identifying and labelling these distractions you'll start to notice when you're doing them more often.'

Overcoming evil becomes a reward in itself, which is precisely what we are doing here with mind monkeys, lizard brains and eating frogs.

What do you feed your monkey?

Your monkey craves quick hits: scratching that itch to check your emails, watching that cat video on Facebook, playing a quick round of Bejeweled. The problem is that these quick hits are like empty calories to your monkey. Monkey gets a quick high and it tastes good but, sooner rather than later, it needs another hit, and then another, then another.

This is especially the case when your work is full of uncertainty. When you are working on that big project or that tricky situation where there is a lot of uncertainty and unknown, the monkey craves certainty. That's why you suddenly get an urge to go and check emails or tidy the stationery cupboard. The urge to do something simple and clearly defined is so tempting, that we crave that bit of certainty, however unnecessary and pointless it may be. And it just gets worse. Just like a sugar addiction, the more instant hits your monkey gets, the more it craves. The more you feed the habit, the more it grows.

Starving your monkey isn't an option. The key is to choose what you feed your monkey. Get it hooked on a diet of real satisfaction and reward and your monkey will happily go along with you to work for the promise of that deeply satisfying feel-good banana it knows it's going to get at the end of the day. But, to do that, you have to hold up your end of the bargain. You have to let your monkey bask in the glory of 'job-done completion'. If you rush straight back to 'what's next' and 'so much to do', your monkey will feel cheated and less likely to come along to play next time. Celebration, achievement and reward matter if you are to keep your monkey playing with you and primed for more.

As well as achievements, your monkey also feeds well on a healthy diet of feeling loved, contributing to a bigger picture and knowing that what it does matters.

MOOD NUDGES

Here are some simple mood nudges that can nourish your monkey:

- Think about three things you are grateful for or, even better, write them down.
- Remind yourself of something bigger which you are a part of – a movement, a community, a team, a family, a faith.
- Hug someone – hugging releases oxytocin, a hormone that is reported to relieve stress, reduce social fears, relieve pain and promote trust, relaxation and compassion. (Note: so does sex, but you might want to be a bit more selective about that.)
- Write down something about yourself that makes you proud.
- Tell someone else why you are proud of them.
- Exercise – get those endorphins moving.
- Get outdoors and stock up on Vitamin D when the sun is out.
- Listen to music that lifts your mood.
- Learn something new.
- Do something just for the fun of it – no targets, no achievement, just have fun.
- Give someone a compliment.
- Give yourself a compliment.
- Perform a random act of kindness.
- Give someone something – a gift, a lift, a smile, your full attention.

- Eat well.
- Make an internal commitment to yourself and honour it. It could be something as simple as take the stairs, smile at someone, turn off your phone or go to bed before midnight.
- Remind yourself you are enough.

Ultimately, an unhappy monkey will act up and cause havoc, while a happy monkey will cheer you on and high-five you as you go.

Don't wake the monkey

Shh... if you are careful, you might not even have to deal with the monkey. Tiptoe around the monkey without waking it. The trick is to avoid sounding the alarm bells that would wake the monkey up. Bells that say **this is a big deal** or **this is going to be hard**!

Baby steps

A really effective way to tiptoe around your monkeys is to take baby steps. Take the big, scary projects that have your mind monkeys screaming and break them down into such small, insignificant steps that your mind monkey opens one eye, rolls over and goes back to sleep.

If you were to tell me five years ago that I would be writing my second book on productivity, I would have laughed and told you that you had the wrong Grace Marshall (as it happens there is another author called Grace Marshall, but she writes erotic fiction – and that's definitely not me!).

You see, I'm naturally disorganised and I have never been good at being on time. So, the fact that my first book topped the Amazon UK ranks for time management still tickles me. Specialising in time management or productivity isn't something I would have chosen myself. If you told me that is what I was setting out to do, I would have run screaming for the hills. But, as a coach working with entrepreneurs who were juggling business and family, the biggest question that always came up was: 'Too much to do, not enough time. How do I fit it all in?' Being a mum of two small children myself, I knew exactly where they were coming from.

Answering that question, one client at a time, and working through it myself, sparked my passion (some would say obsession) with productivity. It wasn't until I was invited to be the Parent Productivity Expert at John William's 'Screw Work Let's Play' programme that I tentatively embraced the 'expert' title and, even then, I kept thinking, 'Any moment now, I'm going to get found out. I'm not the expert they think I'm.'

It turns out that this is a pretty common phenomenon: **imposter syndrome**.

Imposter syndrome describes the fear of being found out; the worry that somehow you don't measure up, that you are not as good as people think you are. Researchers believe that up to 70 per cent of people have suffered from it at some point, including Kate Winslet, Don Cheadle and Maya Angelou. So, I'm in good company.[6]

That is where baby steps come in.

Baby steps mean you don't have to have it all worked out before you start. Instead of telling myself I had to be the expert (cue big alarm bells to summon my mind monkeys), I just focused on helping one person at a time, answering one question at a time. Putting myself out there one little risk at a time.

Baby steps can sneak past fear and confidence wobbles. Do I have what it takes? I don't know. Can I have a go at just this tiny little bit of it? Yes I can. I took the same approach when I started running. As someone who had never been sporty (in fact, I was the girl who was most likely to skive PE at school), the only way to get me running was to start really, really small, to get under the radar of my out-of-shape body and terrified mind. So, I started with 1-minute runs and, within 9 weeks, I was running 5 km non-stop.

Baby steps overcome that feeling of being overwhelmed by making things doable, by breaking down big hairy goals into small, specific steps that you can focus on and absolutely achieve. No ambiguity, nothing else to work out, just plain, simple action.

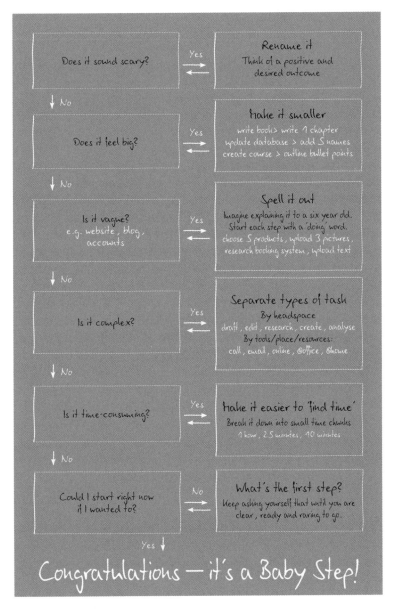

Does it sound scary? — Yes → **Rename it**
Think of a positive and desired outcome

↓ No

Does it feel big? — Yes → **Make it smaller**
write book > write 1 chapter
update database > add 5 names
create course > outline bullet points

↓ No

Is it vague?
e.g. website, blog, accounts — Yes → **Spell it out**
Imagine explaining it to a six year old.
Start each step with a 'doing' word.
choose 5 products, upload 3 pictures,
research booking system, upload text

↓ No

Is it complex? — Yes → **Separate types of task**
By headspace
draft, edit, research, create, analyse
By tools/place/resources:
call, email, online, @office, @home

↓ No

Is it time-consuming? — Yes → **Make it easier to 'find time'**
Break it down into small time chunks
1 hour, 25 minutes, 10 minutes

↓ No

Could I start right now if I wanted to? — No → **What's the first step?**
Keep asking yourself that until you are clear, ready and raring to go.

Yes ↓

Congratulations — it's a Baby Step!

Baby steps checklist

Baby steps bypass procrastination and create momentum, because you actually get started. You take action. It's easy to get started when you are just doing something really simple or really small. And it's easier to keep going, too, to take it one step at a time, rather than cram, crash and burn.

Baby steps also mean you don't have to wait until you have time. It's hard to find time to do a big project, but it's easy to fit in a baby step here and there. I heard a lovely saying the other day that made me smile:

'Even the snail made it to the ark.'

That's how I managed to write my first book in 40 days, around my children, clients and other commitments. And that's how you can, too – whether it's a book you want to write, a mountain you want to climb or a new career you want to break into. Aristotle said, 'We are what we repeatedly do. Excellence, then, is not an act, but a habit.' Extraordinary results come from taking seemingly ordinary steps every day in the right direction.

The art of tinkering

Another way to tiptoe past your mind monkeys without waking them is to tinker, rather than work, on a project. Mark McGuinness, a poet and creative coach, wrote this in an article for *99U*:

'A funny thing often happens when you "just" start setting up and tinkering: you forget about the big, intimidating picture, and start taking small actions that will actually move the project forward. You begin by tweaking and tinkering and, before long, your imagination sparks into life and you're happily absorbed in the work. You've started in earnest without even noticing it.'[7]

This is the process that artists and inventors use to create their best work. They take away the pressure to produce and give themselves permission to play. Some of the best inventions started as play projects, including text messages (SMS), the glue-on Post-it Notes, Blu Tack, bikinis and most of Google's products!

What makes tinkering work so well is the fact that we tell ourselves we're not really working. So there's nothing for your mind monkey to get excited about. Mark Forster, author of *Do it Tomorrow*, suggests that using the words 'I'll just...' can be really powerful to reduce resistance:

'I'm not really going to [the task] right now, but I'll just do [its first step].'

'I'm not really going to write that report now, but I'll just get the file out.'[8]

Try it for yourself:

'I'll just get the file out.'

'It's just another conversation.'

'I'll just scribble a few words.'

'I'll just arrange a meeting.'

'I'll just run it past one person.'

'I'll just answer one question.'

'I'll just see if I can help one person.'

'I'll figure the rest out later. For now I'll just...'

Seven alternatives to being right

My son recently had a meltdown over his homework. His class was transitioning to joined-up handwriting and his homework was to write a set of words in his best joined-up handwriting. Like most things that are new, it feels awkward at first and doesn't come easily.

The more mistakes he made, the more frustrated he got. The more frustrated he got, the more mistakes he made. Eventually, he had a complete meltdown with a whole heap of 'I'm rubbish' and 'I can't do it'. Oh how I miss the days when 'I can't do it' was easily fixed with 'Here, let mummy do it'. Now he's at the age when the learning – and learning the process of learning – is too important to take away from him.

So, we talked about why he was frustrated and it came down to an overwhelming need to get it right. It didn't look neat, therefore it wasn't right, therefore he had failed, therefore he was rubbish. That was his reasoning. That was his monkey's line and he bought it hook, line and sinker. I felt for him – because I know what it's like to be stumped by 'right'. I know what it is like to feel like I have to be right. To feel the pressure to get it right when everyone else around me seems to have it all worked out. Or to be the expert who is expected to have the answers.

But, sometimes, right is the wrong thing to aim for.

Aiming for right can stop us from getting started, when it seems so far from our current reality. It can stop us from stepping into something new, where everything is unknown and uncertain and there is no right. We can become too focused on having to have the right answers that we forget to ask the right questions. We can be so obsessed with right that we forget to have fun.

Sometimes, we have to get things wrong in order to figure out what right even looks like. And sometimes the journey to right looks nothing like right.

Here are some alternatives to being right:

- **Be curious:** embrace the fact that you do not know. Be the one who is asking questions, rather than the one who has all the answers.

- **Be an experimenter:** the one who is testing, rather than the one who is being tested. Experimenting isn't about getting it right. It's just about doing, noticing and learning as you go along.

- **Be a curator:** some of the best 'experts' in the field are actually curators – the people who bring together other people's experience and expertise, who capture the questions and the answers and weave together the stories and the knowledge in such a way that it brings new light to the subject.

- **Be a pioneer:** step out from what you know. Explore the unknown, the place where there is no right. Seek new answers beyond the ones you already have. Go into unchartered territory and see what you discover.

- **Be the fool:** in olden days, the fool, or the jester, could speak the truth to the king when no one else dared. Precisely because they had no authority, agenda or expert status, they could say it exactly how they saw it. They could speak the truth and be heard. There is a freedom that comes with not knowing. With a fresh perspective that is unencumbered by prior knowledge, you can ask the silly questions, address the elephant in the room and bring the breath of fresh air that everyone has been waiting for.

- **Be practising:** sometimes all it takes is practice. Fall down, get up. Try again. Rinse and repeat. I reminded my son that everything he has become good at, everything that now comes naturally to him – from computer games to burping (yes, really!) – was at one point difficult and alien. Sometimes we have to let go of getting it right and just put in the practice. Instead of 'make it look perfect', my son's new goal became 'just fill the page'.

- **Be playful:** our creativity gets stifled when we take ourselves too seriously, when we put too much pressure on getting it right. I experienced this when I started writing this book. I was reminded that 'the best dream to pursue is the one where you enjoy the process as much as the goal'[9] and, dammit, I love writing! I really enjoy it – when I'm not being scared stiff by the high stakes and crazy deadline. I realised I had made my goal so scary, that I had forgotten to have fun, to lose myself in the process of playing with it and trust that process to lead to the right outcome.

Conversations with your monkey

Listen up.

- What is your monkey actually saying?

- What does it need? What your monkey says it needs may not actually be what it needs.

- Is it panicking? Is it standing on a ledge convinced that the building is on fire? Do you need to talk it down?

- Is it insecure? Does it need reassurance and encouragement (rather than entertainment)?

- Is it being a drama queen? Does it need some calm, perspective and normality?

- Is it bored? Does it need some fun, purpose and passion?

- Does it feel backed into a corner? Monkeys tend to see things in black and white. Does it need some alternatives?

- Does it feel threatened? Does it need to know that it's safe to stand down?

- Is it feeling alone or out of its depth? Does it need to ask for support?

The reality check

Is your monkey getting carried away with disaster thinking and tall tales? Here are some tell-tale signs – spot the statements that start with these words:

> They say...
>
> Everyone thinks...
>
> It's always like this...
>
> You never...
>
> No one can...
>
> Nothing will change...
>
> It's all...
>
> That means...

If your monkey is in need of a reality check, here are some questions to ask yourself:

> 'What specifically went wrong?'
>
> 'Who says?'
>
> 'Always?'
>
> 'Never?'
>
> 'Give me a specific example. When has that been the case?'
>
> 'Give me an exception to that. When has that not been the case?'
>
> 'When might it work?'
>
> 'What if it did make a difference? Who would it make a difference to?'
>
> 'What hasn't gone wrong?'
>
> 'What am I making this mean?'

The pep talk

Want to do a great job? Our first job is to put ourselves in a place where we can give our best. That includes the pep talk we give ourselves.

If we let our monkey do the talking, though, it could be a very different conversation!

Ruth was procrastinating on her essay. Experience told her that, if she left it too late, she wouldn't be happy with what she submitted, but the feeling of self-doubt was so strong it was holding her back from getting started. Her monkey had a critical voice:

'I can't do it.'

'I won't be good enough.'

'I'm not academic enough.'

'I'm not disciplined enough.'

As a psychotherapist, on a logical level, she knew that this voice was taking up a huge amount of time and energy: 'And it's not true! And yet I still do it.' She knew there was plenty of evidence to show that she was clearly qualified and equipped to tackle this piece of work, but her monkey wouldn't shut up. She also knew that, if she could just get started, she would find herself enjoying the work. She always did once she got into it. It was just the starting that seemed so damn hard. In fact, once she got started, the hard thing would be stopping!

We decided to give the monkey an opportunity to say its piece. It turned out that there were a couple of essays she had handed in previously that had fair feedback, which she wasn't entirely proud of. She had left them late and didn't feel that she gave them her best shot. Often, our monkeys do speak from a small dose of truth and that's why they are hard to ignore, but they take that small grain of truth and distort and magnify it. Her monkey had decided that it was best to avoid that awful feeling of being judged for as long as possible. It was also quite a heavy and emotional subject matter, and her monkey was also trying to avoid the pain of diving in.

Her response to her monkey was 'that's dreadful!' She could see it wasn't helpful and she kicked herself for thinking it. However, monkeys don't tend to respond well to being kicked or berated. They don't like being told they're dreadful. They tend to act up even more.

So, Ruth decided to do some reframing.

She realised that, by putting off and avoiding doing the research, she was avoiding being judged and fearing that she would be judged to fail – but also not allowing herself to succeed (classic monkey sabotage). So, instead, she decided that, if she was going to be judged anyway, she was going to choose to be judged on what she did do rather than what she didn't do.

She shifted her perspective and focus from how she felt about doing the research, 'I don't know if I'm ready, if I'm good enough, if I have what it takes' to focus on the subject matter, 'this is heavy stuff, this is who it affects, how it happens, how it works, this is what I know about it'. At the same time, she gave herself permission to feel emotional. She invests a lot of her time, energy, heart, soul and headspace into her research so, rather than see it as a sign of weakness or an inability to cope, she accepted that, when the stakes are high, it's perfectly normal to be a bit emotional.

She also decided to change her own critical voice – instead of berating her monkey with 'that's dreadful' and adding to the emotion and drama, instead she simply identified it as 'unhelpful' and 'that's something I'd like to change'. As for the guilt, she realised that, if she was going to give her best, she needed to ask for help to put herself in the best position to focus on the research.

These realisations helped her to focus on the research. By challenging the thoughts that were unhelpful and changing the conversation with her monkey, she shifted the block. Within one week of our conversation, I got this message from her: 'I am now spending no time putting it off and more time enjoying and focusing on the research – Thank you!'

The rant and the reframe

Sometimes, your monkey needs to have a rant, to express its fears and worries and feel listened to. This exercise lets your monkey do just that.

1. Grab two sheets of paper. In the centre of each sheet, write the name of the thing you are resisting, feeling demotivated about or that you are stuck on.

2. On one sheet, give your mind monkey full permission to rant. Get all the unhelpful words and thoughts you have about this out of your head and onto paper. Even if you know it's complete rubbish, if you are thinking it, write it down.

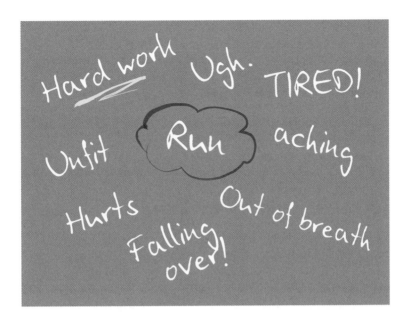

3. On the other sheet, collect and write down all the positive thoughts and helpful words that you associate with this thing.

I find these are most powerful when they come from a place of honesty. So, if you want to write 'easy', but find that your instant reaction is to scoff at it, because you don't quite believe that yet, then try adding 'What if', for example, 'What if it's easier than I think?' or point it in the right direction, e.g. 'getting easier'.

4. Then take a look at each sheet of paper. Notice the difference in how you feel when you look at each one. What you notice grows: the more you notice something, the more of it there is to notice. And that has such an impact on how we experience things. Our thoughts and words shape our perspective. Our perspective shapes our experience. And all of this shapes what we choose to do next.

The beauty of this exercise is that it's all about what's going on in your head, which means you have full control. You can choose which one you focus on. Keep it visible, perhaps at the desk where you work, on the fridge or the mirror, or by your bed. Look at it and let the words soak in – before getting started, before you get up in the morning or even last thing at night. Notice the difference.

Play the 'what if' game

Is your mind monkey saying a lot of 'what if's'? 'What if it goes wrong? What if I fail? What if everybody hates it?'

Is it caught up in catastrophising? 'What if this goes wrong, then... and then... which would lead to...'

What we tend to do goes something along the lines of this:

1. What if: 'What if I mess up the presentation?'.

2. Add meaning: 'I'd look a complete fool, I'd be letting everyone down, I'd lose the sale, my reputation would be in tatters, there's certainly no way I'd be considered for promotion and, with the rumours of restructuring, I might even lose my job...' This stage can last a while!

3. Add evidence: remember that presentation? When you got the slides mixed up and you forgot your words? And that was a friendly audience. Did you hear what happened to the last guy who presented to this audience? They say...

4. Turn 'what if' into 'what is': 'I'm not a speaker. This isn't for me. It's not going to work. This is a terrible idea.'

> **'Worrying is using your imagination to create something you don't want.'**
>
> **ESTHER HICKS, AUTHOR AND SPEAKER**

What if we used our imagination to create what we *do* want instead? The same skill can be used to build faith when we play the 'what if' game in a helpful way:

1. Come up with some positive, helpful 'what-if' statements: 'What if it goes better than I imagine?' 'What if I am good enough?' 'What if it's easier than I think?' 'What if I really enjoy myself?'

2. Add meaning: 'It would be a great experience. I'd land the deal, inspire the team and set a great foundation to build on.'

3. Add evidence: 'Because I've done my research.' 'I've built a good relationship.' 'I'm a good listener.' 'Remember that time I really relaxed into my own shoes and they commented on how naturally I came across?'

4. Turn 'what if' into 'what is': 'I'm good enough because...' 'I will give this my best shot because...' 'This is a great opportunity because...'

Mind your language

There are some words that monkeys seem particularly sensitive to. Simply changing some of those words can change the entire conversation. Here are some common ones:

BUT

'I'm confident in what I do, but running a business/networking/public speaking is all new to me.'

'The website's lovely but the font's too small.'

'I've written 5 chapters, but have 20 more to do.'

'I'm excited, but I'm scared.'

'Ninety-nine happy customers this week, but one complained.'

Notice how 'but' changes the tone of the story? 'We have good news...' Yay! 'But there is bad news...' Oh pants.

'But' has an effect of negating whatever came before. Good news gives way to bad news. Confident becomes not confident. Praise gets overshadowed by criticism. Progress leads to stuck. Done gets replaced by not done. Excited is overwhelmed by scared.

REPLACE BUT WITH AND

'I'm confident in what I do and running a business/networking/public speaking is all new to me.'

'The website's lovely and the font could be bigger.'

'I've written 5 chapters and have 20 more to do.'

'I'm excited and I'm scared.'

'Ninety-nine happy customers and one complaint this week.'

Notice the difference? Both parts of the sentence can exist alongside each other and have equal weight. In fact, the positive statement lends itself to the rest.

'I'm confident **and** this is new.'

'This is great **and** this is how it can be even better.'

'This is what I've done **and** this is what I'm working on.'

'Five down, twenty to go – progress all the way.'

'I'm excited **and** scared – it's ok to be both.'

'Ninety-nine right **and** one wrong – we did well **and** what can we improve?'

Try it! Notice what happens when you say 'and' instead of 'but'.

'-ING' FOR WORK IN PROGRESS

So often we focus on what's done and what's not done. What about the stuff in between? What about the work we are actually doing?

A friend once asked me, 'What are you working on?'. 'How's business?' would have prompted a static answer: great/ good/ok/not bad/could be better/awful/don't ask!

'What are you working on?' prompted a much more enthusiastic response: 'Well, I'm putting together a... and it's really exciting because... I'm still working out... and I'm looking forward to launching it in...'

Progress isn't static. So much of what we do is work in progress: building a business, raising a family, growing in confidence, etc.

What are you working on?

What are you creating?

Where are you growing?

What are you building on?

What are you reaching?

What are you celebrating?

What seeds are you sowing?

What harvest are you reaping?

What reputation or relationships are you building?

What are you transforming?

What results are you seeing?

And when you do take a snapshot and review what is done and complete, where is that leading you?

If you want the momentum and flow of being in progress, make sure your language has plenty of 'ing' in it.

I AM VS. I'M DOING

'I am' speaks to our identity. It feels permanent, part of who we are. 'I'm doing' describes an action, something we are taking part in, at this moment in time, which is temporary and detachable. So, when clients say to me 'I'm a terrible procrastinator', I remind them that procrastination is something you do, not who you are.

We can all **do** procrastination. How do you do yours?

What do you say to yourself or out loud?

What actions do you busy yourself with?

What goes through your mind?

What do you imagine?

Where do you allow your attention to go?

Once we know what we are doing, it becomes much easier to decide what to do differently.

HAVE TO VS. GET TO

'I have to' signals obligation and powerlessness. We have no choice, no control, we are trapped, there's nothing we can do about it. It often gets us playing the victim, 'there's nothing I can do about this' or the rebel, 'what do you mean I have to? No. I'm definitely not going to do it' (cue procrastination).

'I get to' signals opportunity and choice. We can choose, rather than be forced. It gets us looking for reasons why this might be a good thing. Take these examples:

'I have to go to the gym so I can lose weight.'

'I get to go to the gym to lose weight.'

'I have to take the day off because my daughter's sick.'

'I get take the day off to look after my daughter.' (I get to be the one who holds her, to comfort her, I get to give her cuddles.)

Rebekah found that this little change in words completely shifted her perspective. Her business was taking off and she had a lot of work coming in. 'I have all this work to do' was creating a feeling of resentment. She felt bogged down by her workload, deadlines, expectations and obligation. When she started saying 'I get to...' she remembered, 'Hey! I love my work! Look at all these lovely clients I get to work with, and these brilliant projects I get to work on.'

It can even change our perspective on the things we don't have any choice over:

'I have to pay this tax bill.'

'I get to pay a tax bill this year!' (I have actually made enough of a profit to have a tax bill!)

'I have to go to another meeting/make another presentation.'

'I get to influence the decisions and outcomes from this meeting/I get to represent my team and speak up for what we need/I get to get buy in from key stakeholders.'

'I have to deliver the bad news about the restructure.'

'I get to influence how this news is delivered. I get to be on the front lines, supporting and encouraging my colleagues during tough times.'

What are you currently telling yourself you have to do? What would your 'get to' statement be?

CAN'T

When you say 'I can't' what are you really saying? That you don't know how? That you don't have the resources to? That you're not sure you want to? That you are already committed to something else? Sometimes it's easier to say 'can't'.

'I can't make it' is easier to say (and more readily accepted) than 'actually, I'd rather not', 'I'd prefer to do something else' or 'I've already committed to something that I don't want to cancel'.

'I can't possibly do that' is easier to swallow than 'that scares me to death', 'I'm not sure that would work' or, even, 'I don't know how to do that.'

When there is a risk involved, a cost, or a trade-off, 'can't' lets us off the hook. Rather than owning the decision, we default to 'can't' and it's out of our hands. The trouble is, after a while, we believe our 'can'ts' and they become the walls we build that then hem us in. 'Can't' puts us in a position where we feel helpless. It signals impossibility and incapacity – so why bother trying?

I had a couple of conversations recently with friends who have made some pretty radical decisions about their businesses. Decisions they had previously said 'I can't' to.

'I can't take time off.'

'I can't raise my prices.'

'I can't do any more/less.'

'I can't do this in any other way (I've tried… it doesn't work… not for me/my business).'

But something changed when they hit a crisis. One had a health crisis that meant she had to take time off. Another was facing a personal crisis that meant that she had to make some tough choices. Instead of 'I can't', they both found themselves saying, 'This needs to happen. How do I make it happen?'.

All of a sudden, 'I can't' was no longer an acceptable answer. Impossibility was out of the question. Everything was possible and something had to give.

Before, 'I can't' had them utterly convinced that there were no other options. Now, all the rules were thrown out, and they found themselves facing down hard choices, determined to find a way through, making tough decisions with courage, setting boundaries with ruthlessness and letting go of the need to please everybody and get everything right – because 'I can't' wasn't an option any more.

There is something about a crisis that gives us clarity. Clarity over what really matters. What's completely non-negotiable and what's up for grabs. But I wonder if we could create that clarity for ourselves more often, with less crisis, by being more truthful about our 'can'ts'.

Mindset trainer Caroline Ferguson suggests experimenting with this simple language tweak:

When you hear yourself say 'I can't…', try seeing if one of these works instead:
'I choose not to…'
'I haven't yet…'
It sends a completely different message to your brain.

Another alternative to 'I can't' is 'I don't'. For example:

> 'I don't work weekends.'

> 'I don't take calls after 5 pm.'

> 'I don't cancel my gym appointments.'

Give it a try and notice the difference.

Over to you

What's going on in your head? What do *your* mind monkeys get up to?

My mind monkeys are most active when:

....

Their favourite tactics are:

....

What are you going to do about your monkeys?

My monkeys are distracted by: ....

Three things I could experiment with to invite my monkey to play are:

1. ....

2. ....

3. ....

One big/scary project that I could break into baby steps is:

....

Instead of being 'right' I choose to be:

....

Things to stop feeding my monkey:

....

Start feeding my monkey well with:

....

Better conversations to have with my monkey:

....

Words to watch out for:

....

Chapter 4

Fake work vs. real work

> 'Nothing is less productive than to make more efficient what should not be done at all.'
>
> PETER DRUCKER

Ever had a day where you know you've been super busy but, if someone asks you what you got done, you find yourself completely stumped for words?

Being busy isn't hard.

There's always plenty to do. Plenty of emails, calls to make, links to check out, events to research, industry news to keep on top of, requests from colleagues, ideas from your boss (not to mention your own brain), problems to fix, enquiries to answer, people to get up to speed, invoices to chase, someone to cover for, a last-minute opportunity, a long-term project, deadlines that move, meetings to attend, notes to take, information to communicate, presentations to rewrite, data to analyse. Outside of work, there are appointments to make, buttons to fix, food to buy (and cook and clean up after), family to call, favours to do, friends to meet, bills to pay, talks to be had, presents to buy, parties to organise, people to look after, train tickets to collect, etc.

Being busy isn't hard at all. What's hard is knowing what not to do. When do you stop tweaking that manuscript and press send? When do you stop developing your product and actually put it out to market? When do you stop chasing those tiny leads and go for the big fish that scares you? When do you stop being so busy with the fake work and actually get on with the real work?

Some fake work is easy to spot. Some of it feels like genuine hard work. And some real work doesn't feel like work at all. It's time to spot the difference and make some choices about how we really want to spend our time.

Impact thinking

True productivity is knowing what not to do, so you can genuinely commit to what you do do. So, how do you decide? Here are some tools to help you to distinguish between what's worth doing and what is, perhaps, worth less of your effort.

Pareto's Law

The story goes that Pareto was an Italian economist, who was growing peas in his garden. When it came to harvest time, he noticed that 80 per cent of the peas came from 20 per cent of the pods. Like any good economist, he then applied that to everything else in life and found that the same principle holds true. Eighty per cent of a nation's wealth comes from 20 per cent of its population. Eighty per cent of a company's profit comes from 20 per cent of its core customer base, core products or services.

Applying that to the work that you do means that 80 per cent of your results comes from 20 per cent of your actions.

What's your 20 per cent? What's the work that you do that creates far more impact than everything else put together? And what would happen if you focused more of your time, energy and attention on your 20 per cent?

Where to apply this rule

EMAILS

Research suggests that emails can take up to 28 per cent of our working day. How much of this is vital to your work? How much is noise? In the 'Getting Your Inbox to Zero' workshops that I run, we find regularly that the 80/20 rule is more like the 800/20 rule when it comes to emails. For every 20 useful emails that are vital to our work, we get somewhere in the region of 800 emails, which may not be complete spam, but perhaps what we refer to as 'bacon'. These are the somewhat useful, mildly interesting (perhaps even quite tasty) emails that fill our inbox. Common examples of noise we come across are:

- FYI

- CC

- group/global distribution lists
- office announcements: cakes in the kitchen, car parking notices, server maintenance
- out of office/holiday notices
- automatic notifications
- social media updates
- newsgroups
- newsletters
- industry updates
- sales emails.

MEETINGS

Would you be surprised if I told you that 33.91 per cent of all meetings are wasted, that 50 per cent of people find meetings to be unproductive and 9 out of 10 people daydream in meetings? Research suggests that executives spend an average of 23 hours per week in meetings, of which 7.8 hours are unnecessary and poorly run, which equates to 2 months per year wasted![1]

In his humorous, six-minute TED talk, David Grady says:

> 'Every day, we allow our co-workers, who are otherwise very, very nice people, to steal from us... I believe that we are in the middle of a global epidemic of a terrible new illness known as MAS: mindless accept syndrome. The primary symptom of mindless accept syndrome is just accepting a meeting invitation the minute it pops up in your calendar. It's an involuntary reflex – ding, click, bing – it's in your calendar.'[2]

Which meetings can you respectfully decline? Where can you delegate decisions instead of being present to oversee them? 'Here are the parameters. I trust you – just let me know what you decide.'

Ask: 'What's the purpose of the meeting? What do you need from me?'.

David Grady suggests that, when we show people that we are interested in learning how we can help them achieve their goal, and we do this respectfully and often enough, people might start to be a little bit more thoughtful about the way they put together meeting invitations – and we can make more thoughtful decisions about accepting them. If your contribution is needed for only part of the meeting, could you suggest that you attend only that part of the meeting? If you're calling a meeting, could you limit the numbers to only the people who absolutely need to be there? Occasionally, when can you say 'Let's not meet!' and share the information or come to a decision another way?

MARKETING

Are you trying to be all things to all people or do you specialise in what you're really good at? Do you have a focused marketing campaign or are you taking more of a 'spray and pray' scattergun approach? Where does most of your work come from? How could you focus on what works and build on it? What do you need to drop and stop doing to make room for that?

IDEAS

> 'Genius is 1 per cent inspiration, 99 per cent perspiration.'
>
> **THOMAS EDISON**

Ideas are great, but it's only when we pursue them and put in the hard work that we actually create something of value. Saying yes to every idea can be exciting and fun, but it's a sure-fire way to run out of steam and never actually complete anything.

As author Seth Godin challenges, 'Are you a serial idea-starting person? The goal is to be an idea-shipping person.' It's only when you ship it, that it adds value. What good ideas can you say no to so that you can say yes wholeheartedly to the best ideas?

DELEGATING

How much of your time is spent doing something that someone else can do? What is that stopping you from doing?

Action vs. activity

Action takes you forward. Activity keeps you busy. Think about the work you've done in the last week. How much of it actually moved you closer towards your goals? How much of it just kept you busy? Look at your to-do list. How much of it's action and how much is activity? Are you clear which one is which?

Some activity may be critical to keeping the wheels turning – your day-to-day job, delivering on existing commitments, keeping things going as they are. But if your wider mission is to transform the business, move into a new market, get that promotion or qualification, go freelance or simply work less, then your actions are the ones that actually move you towards that goal.

You may not be able to eliminate all your activity (and, indeed, you might not want to) but if you don't seem to be making progress on any of your actions, perhaps you need to eliminate some of your activity to make space for the actions that matter to you.

How much time do you spend on keeping everything ticking over rather than moving you forward?

What's in a name?

Project names can also help us identify what's worth doing. How often do you label your projects with generic names such as 'Website', 'Marketing' or 'Admin'? What does that do for your focus, clarity and motivation? Here are four common pitfalls of having a generic project name:

1. **There is no defined outcome.** How do you know when you've got there? It's hard to stay focused when you've got no finish line to focus on. And it's hard to get that job-done sense of satisfaction, or even a sense of progress, when you don't have a clue what 'done' looks like.

2. **It becomes a dumping ground.** Without a defined focus, generic projects such as 'Website' can become an easy catch-all bucket for any tasks, thoughts or ideas that are remotely website related, but don't actually come together towards a common goal. This means you either end up busily ticking things off with no real sense of direction or you get so overwhelmed that you shut the door on your dumping ground and turn your attention to something more manageable instead.

3. **There's plenty of room for project creep.** You start off with plans for a simple website to showcase your expertise. Then you decide to add a blog and a shopping cart... and some social media integration. This means you need to revive your Twitter account... what about Pinterest? Maybe you'll add an interactive forum to the website, get people engaged... and, really, you should have some video...

   All these, potentially, are good ideas, but it doesn't matter how big the project grows: if you're not shipping anything and if that simple website remains unlaunched, none of it makes any difference.

4. **It's boring.** Generic project names often feel boring, heavy, serious and too much like a chore, like Maths homework. Just thinking about it makes you groan and look for the nearest light relief to procrastinate with.

   That's the reason why I renamed my admin project 'Engine Room'. Admin makes me want to run a mile, whereas 'Engine Room' reminds me that this is the stuff that keeps my business running and ticking over. It may not be pretty, and I might have to get my hands dirty, but it's sure-as-heck vital if I want to carry on playing above deck, and that gives me the motivation to roll up my sleeves and get stuck in, elbow deep, to accounts and paperwork.

What about you? Do you have any generic projects on the go at the moment? Try renaming them. Think of a positive, desired outcome. Be clear, be decisive and be playful – choose a name that excites you – and see what that does for your focus and momentum.

Here are some great project names that I've come across:

- Reclaim living room

- Home sweet home

- Enjoy Christmas

- Revive team spirit

- Make Sally laugh

- Wonderful work place

- Make the boat go faster[3]

- (add yours here):

....

The perfectionist's curse

> 'The last moments spent on anything are rarely the most valuable.'
>
> **GRAHAM ALLCOTT, HOW TO BE A PRODUCTIVITY NINJA**

The curse of the perfectionist is that we know exactly what perfect looks like but never quite attain it, while good enough is attainable, but kind of hard to define. Somewhere between good enough and nearly-but-never-quite-perfect is the territory where real work becomes fake work. Where thinking becomes overthinking. Analysing becomes over-analysing. Writing becomes excessive. Checking becomes obsessive.

What makes it difficult to tell is that every extra ounce of effort we put in probably does create a tiny drop of real value, but the closer we get to perfect, the more effort it takes and the less value it creates. It's up to us to work out the pay-off. Do I spend all day getting this perfect? Or do I spend half the time doing a good enough job, then move on to the next thing?

Athletes at the top of their game probably spend an inordinate amount of time perfecting their sport but in order to do this there will be other things they need to do to a much lower standard. We can achieve extraordinary things as long as we accept other things to be ordinary. We can certainly excel in a few choice things, but not everything can be – or needs to be – done to a gold-plated standard. Some things are fine being silver-plated, bronze-plated or just plain done.

Your choice.

Less is more

Great editors and designers know that what they remove adds value to what remains. Saying less sometimes can have a bigger impact. An unhurried cup of tea can be far more pleasurable than an elaborate banquet. Doing one thing well can bring far more satisfaction than doing a hundred things badly. A five-sentence email gets read and replied to far more quickly than an essay. A three-minute video can be much more memorable than a three-hour lecture. In our crowded lives, space is the thing we hunger for more than things.

The new normal

How often do we answer the question 'How's it going?' with 'Busy!'? Busyness has become the norm. But it has also become strangely aspirational. As much as we complain about being busy, we are also strangely resistant to being not busy.

When was the last time you heard anyone admitting to not being busy? That they had plenty of time, things were nice and slow and they had plenty of spare capacity? Why are we afraid of the alternative? What would it mean to be not busy? Does that mean I'm lazy? Not doing enough? Will someone come and give me more work to do?

For those who run our own businesses, busy is seen often as a measure of success. Busy means you're in demand, therefore you must be doing something right. If you're not busy, what have you done wrong? Is your product substandard? Is your service poor? Have you neglected your marketing?

For those who work in busy organisations, admitting to not being too busy might land you with more work to do. You're on top of your work, are you? Great – go and help Sally with her backlog! Or, worse, maybe someone will start questioning whether you are surplus to requirements...

We might even feel resentment if someone is not busy – that somehow they're not pulling their weight. If the rest of us are suffering, surely they should be carrying their piece of the burden, too?

We validate our worth with busy. There's something about being busy that gets associated with being wanted, being needed, being in demand. Honestly, there is a part of me that enjoys being busy. I feel useful.

We use busy to judge whether we decide to do something or not – it seems more acceptable (or at least easier) to say, 'no, sorry I'm busy' than to say 'thanks, but no thanks'.

We satisfy ourselves that we are doing the best we can because we are busy and couldn't possibly do any more. Or we feel like a constant failure because we're so busy trying to catch up.

Busy is seen as a good work ethic. And those who are not busy are viewed with suspicion.

Busy is our means of achieving, but also our excuse for not achieving. Not dealing with that problem that we've been avoiding. Not making that appointment to get that lump checked out. Not taking a break or booking that holiday you keep promising yourself. Not going for that run, that swim or that walk. Not having that difficult conversation with your partner, your boss or your kids. Not cutting your losses on the project that's not working out. Not letting go of that customer you have outgrown. Not being ruthless and saying no...

We know what we need to do to manage our stress and stay healthy, but we don't do it because we're too busy. As the American Psychological Association's 'Stress In America' 2010 report found:[4]

> 'In general, Americans recognize that their stress levels remain high and exceed what they consider to be healthy. Adults seem to understand the importance of healthy behaviours like managing their stress levels, eating right, getting enough sleep and exercise,

but they report experiencing challenges practicing these healthy behaviours. They report being too busy as a primary barrier preventing them from better managing their stress...'

Dr Susan Koven of Massachusetts General Hospital wrote in her 2013 *Boston Globe* column:[5]

'In the past few years, I've observed an epidemic of sorts: patient after patient suffering from the same condition. The symptoms of this condition include fatigue, irritability, insomnia, anxiety, headaches, heartburn, bowel disturbances, back pain, and weight gain. There are no blood tests or X-rays diagnostic of this condition, and yet it's easy to recognize. The condition is excessive busyness.'

How does this play out in your workplace?

Do you honour the person who stays the latest or works the longest? Is there an unofficial competition for who has the largest to-do list? Mixed in with the sympathy, is there a certain sense of importance or admiration (or kudos) for the person who does the most?

Do we secretly (or not so secretly) think more of the person who always says yes? Do we hold the mantra that 'if you want something done, give it to a busy person'?

Does your workplace have an unspoken culture of honouring the person who leaves the office the latest?

Why not turn that around? Celebrate the person who does their best work in the fastest time, instead of the one who takes the longest. Give people the freedom to clock off early when they've had a super-productive day. Measure work done by impact and results, rather than face-time.

> **TIP**
>
> Decide what 'job done' looks like at the beginning of the day. Give yourself a short, closed list to work from, then, when you get to the bottom, consider your

day's work done. Whatever time you have left over is yours to use as you choose. If you choose to work more, then consider that a bonus, over and above what was required for the day. If you choose to take the time off, do it with complete satisfaction that you have earned it.

Fake work

Some fake work is easy to spot: watering the plants, staring into space, fiddling with the spreadsheet, designing yet another trifold brochure, spending hours reading non-important emails.

Some feels like genuine hard work, and it is, but maybe that's all it is: hard work that doesn't take you anywhere; hard work that just keeps your wheels spinning, going nowhere fast; hard work that keeps you busy rather than moves you forward.

Fake work could be:

- working on the fifth iteration of the new brochure rather than picking up the phone to that customer

- perfecting your business card instead of going out networking

- doing more research when you know you should be delivering

- adjusting the font or rereading just one more time instead of pressing publish

- playing email ping pong instead of picking up the phone

- dancing around a subject instead of getting to the point

- building another spreadsheet model instead of getting investors in

- having another meeting instead of making the decision

- weighing in with your opinion on another colleague's problem, instead of working on what you really need to figure out

- offering a quick fix instead of really listening to what someone wants

- spending way too long doing a post-mortem analysis instead of moving on with a quick fix

- rewriting your to-do list

- making a list of people to call

- analysing who to call (until you run out of time to call them).

Ditching the fake work – removing the temptation

My friend and Chief Ninja Graham Allcott has a theory that productivity is a battle between the two very different versions of you: the lazy, scatterbrained you versus the clever, motivated you. The lazy, scatterbrained you jabs away at you, distracting you, tempting you, wearing you down, but the clever motivated you can deliver some pretty strong sucker punches that can disarm the lazy scatterbrained you. These are known as power moves:

- Deactivating your Facebook account or installing a social media blocker during work hours is a power move that saves you having to resist lots of moments of temptation to check during the day.

- Turning email notifications off on your phone and desktop is a power move that saves all those pings and pop ups calling to you.

- Putting your phone on charge downstairs and getting an old-fashioned alarm clock is a power move that removes the temptation to take your work to bed.

- Setting a deadline and making yourself publicly accountable is a great way of putting a limit on your procrastination and perfectionism. A deadline in someone else's world makes a target much more real and powerful.

- Outsourcing the work you secretly quite enjoy doing but know that you need to release is a power move that reduces the temptation to do it all yourself. If you're paying for someone else to do it, you're less likely to double up on the work.

When does preparation become procrastination?

When it replaces the work instead of enabling it.

This is how author Janice Horton described her writer's procrastination:

> 'I tend to get immediately side-tracked on my way to my desk and I find that I'm giving other jobs (housework or cooking mostly) priority over what I should be doing (writing my books). It's as if I have to get the other things out of the way, in order to "clear my mind and my workspace" and concentrate fully on my writing. Often, by the time this happens, I'm physically and mentally tired!'

Clearing space, both mentally and physically, to work can be a really useful thing. But when it takes over and replaces your work, that's not so helpful! The truth is, there's always stuff to do. There is always another job to do, another pile to tidy, another thing to remember, another email to answer. If you wait until everything is done before you start writing, you will never start.

The same goes for that pile of emails, meeting notes or colleague requests you feel compelled to clear out of the way, before you start on your own work. Or the amount of research you want to do before you feel confident presenting your idea to your boss.

The trick is to limit your preparation. Give yourself, say, 15–30 minutes to get your space in order. This will get you deciding what absolutely needs to be in place during that time (e.g., pen, paper, laptop, cup of tea, urgent disasters averted) and what can wait until later (e.g., the report for next week's meeting, phoning the bank, replying to emails). Use a timer if you need to.

Remember, preparation enables work. Procrastination replaces it.

Real work

Just as fake work can sometimes feel a lot like work, real work sometimes doesn't feel like work at all. Often, what keeps us busy is that we don't give ourselves permission to do what doesn't feel like work, for example.

Thinking time

As one workshop delegate put it: 'I always feel like I'm wasting time when I stop and think. I feel like I should just get on with it.' But thinking is where we define the work, decide the what, when, why and how of work. Thinking can make all the difference between a productive day and a busy day, between meaningful work and meaningless chore, between us doing the work and the work doing us.

Recharge time

Whether it's time to rest, have fun, indulge or let your mind freewheel, if it recharges you and restores your capacity to do your best work, it could be the most productive thing you can make time for. As human beings, we are not designed to function non-stop without a break. Our brains get bored, tired and lose focus. We stop being able to do our best work, to think strategically, logically and creatively and, instead, just go through the motions.

The problem is that taking a break feels unproductive. And the part of us that subscribes to the busy culture tells us we are slacking. We feel guilty. In a study commissioned by Staples, a study of office workers and managers revealed that, even though an overwhelming majority of workers (86 per cent) acknowledge that taking a break would make them more productive and 90 per cent of employers say they encourage breaks, more than a quarter of workers do not take a break other than lunch and one in five employee respondents cites guilt as the reason they don't step away from their workspaces.

Asking silly questions

I used to hate asking questions for fear of making a fool of myself and wasting someone else's time. Now I have learnt to start with, 'Can I ask a silly question?' and the answer is always yes. More often than not, it's not a silly question at all. If nothing else, it gives me clarity instead of confusion. And, once in a while, the blindingly obvious turns out to be brilliantly helpful.

Letting someone else do it more slowly... or, even, badly

When my children insist on doing things themselves – their shoelaces, seatbelt, reaching the cereal box, finishing their own sentences, I have to admit there are times I'm tempted to take over, especially when we're already running late. Sometimes I do give in and take over, but the more I can give them time to do it for themselves, the more they learn and the more independent they become. As my husband says, our ultimate job as parents is to make ourselves redundant. The same goes for delegating. The early days of letting someone else learn the ropes are painful. It's great when others can do what they can do, so you can do what only you can do, but getting there takes time.

Blank space in the diary

When time is limited, it's tempting to cram something into every nook and cranny, the way a budget airline packs people in like sardines. It feels inefficient to leave gaps. But gaps give us room to manoeuvre and margin to adapt to the unexpected. Building margin into our day is precisely the thing that helps us to stay productive in a fast-changing, unpredictable world. And if you've had the budget airline experience, you will know that breathing space itself adds massively to the quality of our day.

More than what you do

If you are a teacher, how you show up in the classroom will affect how you inspire those children and what kind of role model you become. As a speaker, the energy you bring into the room and how you deliver your talk will affect what people take away. Your job is more than what you do. You are more than what you do. The value you bring, your life's work, your immediate impact and your lasting legacy depend as much on who you bring into the room as what you do.

What are you building?

Everything we do does two things: there is the thing we do and there is the thing we build. For example, saying yes to one job builds your reputation in that area. Every job you do builds your reputation. Is that the direction you want to build your career or business?

Answering the question for the fifth time answers the question. But it also creates a precedent. It makes you more likely to be the oracle in your organisation – the person people are likely to turn to before they ask Google. Responding to an email on a Sunday afternoon may be a one-off thing, but it also sends a signal that you may be accessible on a Sunday afternoon and that can start to build an expectation. Every act builds a habit. And when individual habits come together, they become culture.

The fine art of faffing

> *'Faff about/around*: to spend your time doing a lot of things that are not important instead of the thing that you should be doing.'
> **CAMBRIDGE ONLINE DICTIONARY**[6]

Let's face it, we can all do it: that quick check of your emails, the quick water-cooler conversation, the cat videos, hanging around on social media a bit too long, popping in next door – or at the next desk – for a quick catch up, making a list, making a cup of tea, changing the list, tweaking the font, making it look pretty, changing your mind, opening up that project, rearranging the papers, putting them down again, making another cup of tea, checking your phone, checking your email, checking the brief again, seeing if anything has changed...

They say that fight or flight is our body's natural response to stress. I reckon freeze and faff are also in there somewhere. Sometimes, when the workload is high, our response is to faff. To feel like we are doing something, because the thought of doing nothing is unbearable, but the thought of doing **the** thing is too painful.

There are times when we do need to just stop it. Stop faffing around. Close down Facebook. Turn off the internet. Put away that magazine. Turn off your phone. Lock yourself in a room. Tell your friends not to talk to you until that thing is done.

But let's not fool ourselves. We can't spend 100 per cent of our time in high-production, high-performance mode. And, indeed we shouldn't.

True productivity is about harnessing the highs and the lows, not coasting on mediocrity.

So, if we're going to faff anyway, let's master the fine art of faffing.

Productive procrastination

There are times when our brains just need a break. When staring at the screen is blatantly not working. If you're going to procrastinate, you might as well procrastinate well.

Two projects on the go

My friend Marianne often works with two projects on the go. When one feels too heavy or boring, she flips over to the other one. Her mind monkey is happy because it thinks she's procrastinating. The other project is a playground to avoid doing the work. When that project starts to feel too much like hard work, she switches back to the first one. By bouncing around between the two, she never feels forced to work and always makes progress, whether she feels like she's working or not.

Pick and mix

I love it when my husband works from home. Miraculously, all the little jobs that have been hanging around for weeks suddenly get done: the door handle that needs fixing, the bulb that needs replacing, the car part that needs ordering, the lawn that needs mowing... (sadly, not the edging on the living room floor, though). Because when he's procrastinating, he looks for something useful to do; something not too taxing, something that gives him a quick hit, preferably something physical if his brain is tired.

Sometimes, switching between the large tasks and quick wins or different types of tasks can be incredibly effective. If I've spent ages typing away and I'm craving some human contact, all of a sudden that follow-up call I've been putting off doesn't seem so bad after all. If I need a break from mental heavy lifting, doing some brain-dead filing is perfect. If staring at a spreadsheet is making me woozy, going for a walk and taking one of my thinking tasks with me is a great way to restore my sanity and my focus. If my brain is done for the day, batch cooking a few meals for the week ahead makes me feel positively virtuous.

The trick is to have this stuff ready to pick up when you need to. Keep your quick-win files to hand, or your tool box by your desk. Use categories such as @thinking or @zombie in your to-do list to batch up these kinds of tasks so you can access them easily when you need to switch focus – instead of accidentally ending up on YouTube watching cat videos or at your colleague's desk discussing the football or election results.

Your pick-me-up playlist

What do you do when you're feeling fed up? When you look at your to-do list and feel a bit 'meh'? Do you find yourself stuck in limbo land, trudging away half-heartedly, not really working but not not working either? Do you drag yourself to your seat, only to stare at the screen for an hour? Or do you do something that picks you up and gets you back on track?

Something I encourage my clients to do is to put together a pick-me-up playlist – a list of energisers that boost your mood, kick-start your motivation and get you inspired and moving again.

They could be big things or little things. In fact, I find tiny things work exceptionally well. They could include, but are definitely not limited to:

Music: I have an actual pick-me-up playlist on Spotify of all the tunes that get me smiling and dancing. You know, the ones that come on in the car that get you belting away (and possibly driving that little bit faster).

Fresh food: instead of reaching for the nearest comfort junk. When I'm feeling run down and sorry for myself, I have been known to stalk the supermarket staff with the reduced ticket machine down the fruit and veg aisle, loading up fresh vegetables to make soup. Even the act of putting it into my basket makes me feel better, let alone eating it. Likewise, as much as I love my coffee, it's water that gets my brain cells working properly.

Getting outside: for a walk, a run or just a breath of fresh air. One week, in between the ice storms, floods and tornados, there was a rare moment when the sun was streaming across the fence of my garden. I literally stuck my head outside, faced the sun, closed my eyes and basked – like the Disney character Wall-E – for a couple of minutes. Who knew you could sunbathe in the middle of February in England?

Activities: for me, it's conversations. Being a people person, inspiring conversation to me is like rocket fuel, which is why 'phone a friend' is on my list of pick me ups, as well as connecting with people I haven't even met – bloggers, writers and TED talkers – who inspire me. Taking a break to read or listen to something that inspires me can do far more for my muse than staring at a blank screen.

What about you? What would be on your pick-me-up playlist? Don't wait until you need it. Start now. When you're feeling fed up, that's the worst time to try and come up with something inspiring. Start compiling your playlist now, add to it when something else inspires you and then, when you need to, you can simply pick something and press play.

Wasted time

> 'Time you enjoy wasting is not wasted time.'
> **BERTRAND RUSSELL**

I spotted this on a sign in a shop once. Sometimes, the thing that keeps us trudging along in busy mode is the fact that we feel guilty if we're wasting time.

But, actually, if it's time we truly enjoy spending – daydreaming, napping, chatting, doing nothing – and it restores our capacity to do good, worthwhile, meaningful work, then perhaps it's not wasteful at all.

At the end of the day, our time will feel productive only if what we're spending it on is personally meaningful. What is productivity, after all, if it's not about making space for what matters?

If we tick lots of things off the list that don't matter to us, will that feel satisfying?

If we meet with lots of people but can't remember a single conversation, is that meaningful?

If we make lots of money but never get to spend it, is that truly valuable?

If we have time (and we do) but never enjoy it, frankly what's the point?

When you get to the end of the day, instead of asking yourself 'What have I done?' try asking yourself:

'What am I proud of?'

'What did I especially enjoy?'

'What did I relish?'

'What am I grateful for?'

'What made a difference?'

'What surprised me?'

'What were the moments that mattered?'

No one can tell you what's your fake work and what's your real work. Only you can decide. Real work feeds you. It gives you a sense of satisfaction that you're contributing to something that matters to you. Fake work steals your energy and your time and gives you very little in return.

It's up to you to decide which is which in your world and how much of your life you devote to each.

Where do you find yourself too busy? How much of your time and energy is spent on fake work vs. real work?

Over to you

What's your relationship with busy?

How I stay busy:

....

How we honour busy at work:

....

One thing I can do to start changing this:

....

Impact thinking

My 20 per cent – this is where I make my biggest impact:

....

Action that moves me forward:

....

Activity that keeps me busy:

....

What can I do less of? What can I be ruthless with?

....

One thing I can drop or delegate this week:

....

Fake work vs. real work

Fake work to watch out for:

....
....
....

One power move to reduce the temptation to do fake work:

....
....
....

Real work to make space for:

....
....
....

One thing I'm going to do differently to make space for more real work:

....
....
....

My pick-me-up playlist (if I'm going to procrastinate I might as well procrastinate well!):

....
....
....
....
....
....
....
....

Chapter 5

Real-world tactics: how to be productive when the rest of the world isn't

In an ideal world, we'd get ourselves perfectly organised, know exactly what we need to do, be 100-per-cent focused, get it done and go home. In the real world, however, we have to work with and around other people's priorities, schedules, expectations, delays and last-minute emergencies. What conversations can we have to set expectations and influence others? How can we equip ourselves to respond with calm and agility rather than react with our back against the wall?

In reality, none of us works in a bubble. We work with other people. We rely on other people in order to get our work done well: colleagues, co-workers, customers, suppliers, partners, bosses, staff, stakeholders – and everyone has their own agendas, priorities, schedules, expectations and ways of working. We also work in imperfect situations: project deadlines that were way too tight to begin with, emergencies we failed to scope, delays we didn't plan for, curveballs and changes beyond our control.

What tactics can we put in place to help the day-to-day stuff work better? What uncommon conversations could we be having more often to ensure we have a common focus instead of taking each other off track? And how do we respond when mistakes happen and stuff hits the fan?

Day-to-day tactics

It's one thing getting yourself organised and focused, but what about everyone else in the office? Here are some day-to-day tactics I have come across that can improve workplace productivity.

Do not disturb

'Is now a good time? Have you got a minute?' Well no, not really, but you've got my attention now, so 'Sure, how can I help?' you say.

Open offices can be great for collaboration, social interaction, building relationships and creating an energising buzz to work in, but they can also be the number-one killer of focused attention. The problem is there's no easy way to tell whether it's a good time or not, unless you have mastered the do-not-disturb glare – but, even then, you still need to spot them coming. In the days when we all worked in separate offices, we could close the door as a do-not-disturb signal. Nowadays, with open offices, perhaps we need to be a bit more creative.

Think Productive's chief operating officer, Elena, has a china cat that she puts on her desk when she needs to have some uninterrupted time to herself. When the cat is on the desk, it's her way of saying, 'I need to focus right now. Unless it's an emergency, could you come back later, please?'. When the cat is not there, she is happy to be interrupted. Other people use headphones, traffic-light signals, flag systems, signs or even hiding behind a plant.

The key to making this work is communication. If we expect our colleagues to be mind readers and to **know** what our signals mean, then we are setting ourselves up for disappointment – as well as the frustration and irony of having to stop what we're doing to explain that we didn't want to be disturbed. Instead of demanding mind reading, explain that there are times when you need to have your brain to yourself, when you're unlikely to be able to give anyone else your best attention or your best answer. Show them what you're going to use as a do-not-disturb signal, instead of expecting them to guess, and reassure them that there will be times when you will be fully available. Have a conversation that might start with something like this:

'If the building's burning down, do interrupt me! But if it's not an emergency, and I've got my headphones on, could you just hold that thought and come back to me later? When the headphones are off, I'm all yours.'

You may find, when you have this conversation, that it prompts or gives others permission to do the same. We all have times when we need to have our brains to ourselves – you might just start a trend in the office! If you find it takes a little while for people to get used to it, give it time. It takes time and practice for people to get used to a new way of working. Don't let one person's 'I forgot' deter you. Some people may need a little bit more training than others.

What could you use as a do-not-disturb signal for those times when you really need to get your head down and focus?

> **TIP**
>
> If you use an internal messaging system such as Lync, you can set your status to 'do not disturb' – which means that you can still send Instant Messages, but others can't initiate a conversation with you. If there are a select few you want to give the power to override that 'do not disturb' to, change your privacy relationship with those contacts to 'Workgroup'.[1]

Stealth and camouflage

There may be times when you do need to hide away, rather than have a do-not-disturb signal at your desk. This is where tactical hiding can be quite handy.

Physically being out of the office or away from your desk can give you that extra space and, for some people I've worked with, it's the only way to ensure they get to focus their attention on their own agenda, rather than responding to others. As we'll explore more in Chapter 6, we all need a combination of being available for ourselves and to others. In the meantime, where could you practise some stealth and camouflage? In a meeting room, working from home, or at another office? In a café, at an art gallery or the local library?

However, if you're going to disappear for a while you might want to communicate this so everyone knows what to expect. Otherwise, if you develop a reputation for being too hard to find, it could backfire on you and you could end up playing an elaborate game of corporate hide and seek instead.

Chief Ninja Graham Allcott once sent an email to tell us that he was going to be 'off the grid' for a week to write his book:

Hi all,

Just a quick note to say next week I'm going dark, to write a big chunk of the 'Introducing Productivity' book.

So I'll be off all social media, email and phone for the whole week. I'm around all of this week if you need stuff though.

And then back on Monday 3rd March.

Graham

Instead of just disappearing off the face of the earth, he gave us advance notice and made himself available the week beforehand so that if there was anything we needed to talk about, we could raise it before he disappeared. As it happened, there was something I needed to discuss with him. In my own timing I would have waited until the next week to raise it with him, but knowing his timing I was able to schedule a meeting before he 'went dark', resulting in no delays for my project and plenty of uninterrupted space to write for Graham.

Electronically unplugging is another form of stealth and camouflage. While Graham has managed to practise stealth and camouflage in style – he wrote most of his Ninja books on a beach in Sri Lanka – I have had to be a little bit more DIY with mine. My last book was written largely at my kitchen table and this one in a café, in slightly less sunny Stafford, around children, clients and other commitments.

My way of creating stealth and camouflage is by electronically unplugging: turning off email and social media and putting my phone on 'Do not Disturb' (a lovely setting on my iPhone, which means I can still receive calls from my husband and the children's school, but divert everything else to voicemail). I even used social media as my accountability tool, declaring 'Unplugging for the next hour to write another chapter on my book', knowing full well that each status update is time-stamped, so the eagle-eyed on Twitter would call me out if they saw me online within the hour. This would also work well with instant messaging systems such as Lync and Skype: 'Working on Project X today between 10.00 and 12.00. Back in communication this afternoon.'

The daily huddle

The head-office team at Think Productive has a daily huddle at 9:40 am, where they meet for 10 minutes and ask each other:

- What's your good news?

- What are you working on?

- Where are we up to with the numbers and targets in the business?

- What are we stuck on?

- Are we ok for tomorrow's call – is anyone not here tomorrow?

It's great for bringing everyone together, reminding them what's most important and encouraging good communication. It often flags up any hot potatoes, things that need further discussion, opportunities for collaboration and who might need some extra help that day.

Agendas

Paula is our Client Happiness and Logistics Manager. She handles all the logistics of booking-in workshops. Whenever I want to check in on the status of one of my workshop bookings, I can call her up or send her an email – except I'm not the only person whose workshops she manages. So, if we all called her to check on the status of our workshops, Paula wouldn't have a chance to get any work done!

So I keep an agenda for Paula. Roughly once a week, we'll talk on the phone and find out where things are up to with each of my bookings, if there are any questions I need to answer, further information to provide or people I need to nudge. I rely on Paula to tell me if she needs me to look at anything before we speak.

When there is someone you work closely with, it's easy to get into the habit of firing off questions when they come to mind and you can end up constantly interrupting each other.

Instead, keep a running agenda of all the things you want to discuss with them and ask them to do the same. That way, rather than interrupting each other throughout the day, when you speak you have a list of everything you want to ask or discuss.

Who can you keep an agenda for? Who can you suggest this to?

Project updates

Why do we have update meetings? Seriously, what's the point? The worst ones are where everyone just has their say – where everyone's agenda is just to fill their slot with some kind of an update – usually along the lines of 'this is what I've been busy doing'. But what does 'Can I have an update?' even mean?

Dr Penny Pullan of Making Projects Work says,[2]

> **'The most effective project updates are about two-way communication, not just pushing out information. They ensure that people know what they need to know and can feedback to you. There are no nasty surprises! First of all, you need to understand who you're updating. What does success for your project mean to them? What are their communication needs?'**

The accountant's definition of success may well be different from the marketing director's and, as such, they will want to know different things. People have different preferences, depending on their personal style and level of involvement. Where one person might want a detailed briefing each week, someone else may want only the headlines once a month. Knowing those expectations upfront can make your life easier (less mind reading!) and your updates more meaningful.

A communication plan essentially boils down to these factors:

- Who needs what?

- By when?

- What format?

- How often?

- Are you going to keep records?

Once you know this, you can decide what an update could look like – for example, a super-quick update, a more comprehensive update or something visual.

THE SUPER-QUICK UPDATE

- Here's what we achieved last Friday, last week, etc.

- Here's what we're doing now.

- Please help us with...

- What questions do you have?

THE MORE COMPREHENSIVE UPDATE

- Progress: what's done, what's on track, what's changed, what's next.

- Impact: what this means for you.

- Requests: what I need from you/please help us with...

- Next actions: who's doing what next.

- Questions: what questions do you have?

- Next check-in: already in the diary/arrange date in diary now.

GET VISUAL

Your update might not even be full of words. Sometimes visual cues can be far more effective than lengthy documents or meetings. For example, the London 2012 Olympic Games update consisted of a single A3 colour sheet that showed the status of multiple projects, using traffic-light colours to track the performance of each project: red (significant issues), amber (potential problems that need attention) and green (going as planned).

How else could you give your update and invite questions? A three-minute video? A walking meeting? An internal client/project management system?

Uncommon conversations

One of the things I love seeing from workshops is the level of new conversations that come out of the discussion, as people are challenged to think differently, not just about their own individual habits, but about how they work together as a team. Here are some of the best conversations that I have seen teams take forward from their workshops.

What do we need to let go of?

'Listen up guys, we've got a new client/project/opportunity...'

New opportunities come up, new clients, new projects, new ideas. Reviewing and setting new expectations is part of everyday working. 'There's more work' is probably a conversation we are very used to having. But how often do we talk about releasing expectations? How often do we deliberately talk – with ourselves or with our team – about what we should stop doing and what we should ditch to make space for what we've taken on?

One of my favourite sayings is:

> **'You can't reach for anything new if your hands are still full of yesterday's junk.'**
>
> **LOUISE SMITH, NASCAR RACER, KNOWN AS THE 'FIRST LADY' OF RACING**

But sometimes what we hold onto isn't necessarily junk. It might be the product that sells but is not particularly profitable, the legacy project that's not quite failing but, equally, isn't going anywhere fast, or the campaign or event you've always done that doesn't really line up with your current vision.

What do we need to release? What do we need to be ruthless with?

How much of this problem are we creating, contributing towards or reinforcing?

Are you always working with your back up against the wall? Has firefighting become normality? Sometimes we accept things just as they are without really thinking about them.

One of the lightbulb moments I really enjoy seeing, when running workshops with teams, is when the conversation changes from 'how do we cope with all this relentless work?' to 'how much of this are we creating for ourselves?'.

When one sales-team leader speaks up and says, 'Yes, we do spend a lot of our time chasing the 80 per cent instead of focusing on the 20 per cent' it opens up the conversation and gives permission for the rest of the team to challenge their collective focus.

When the web designer, whose customers always frustrate her by leaving things to the last minute, realises that, with the right conversations and pre-planning, she can proactively manage her clients and give them a nudge, that does wonders for their own project management: 'Oh, thanks for the prompt! I've been meaning to get in touch with you about that', as well as her own planning.

Or when the head of department realises that every email he sends generates more inbound traffic, and every time he replies 'out of hours', he reinforces the expectation that he is available out of hours – and sets an unintended expectation for the rest of the department too.

What is hampering your productivity or your team's productivity at the moment? How much of it have you created for yourselves, do you contribute to or perpetuate with your own working habits? The beauty of being involved in creating the problem means that you're in a great place to be part of the solution.

What do you want... and what do you need from me?

What do you do when you're the person that everybody turns to? The oracle who knows everything and everyone? The problem solver that everyone wants in their meeting? The natural helper who can always be relied on to help you out of a pickle? The unofficial counsellor – the wise voice of reason who talks you out of hitting someone or gives you a shoulder to cry on? Or the boss people turn to for direction, decisions and authority?

It can be flattering and a real honour to be the person that other people turn to when they need help, but it can also be tricky to be the go-to person when you've got a lot on your own plate.

One university lecturer I spoke to told the story of a dean who would regularly arrive to find a queue of people outside his office wanting to ask for his expertise, decision, authority or influence; people who wanted him to help them solve a problem. Before he let them through the door, they had to answer two questions:

- What do you want?

- What have you already done about this?

He wanted to make sure that they had already done the ground work – that not only had they clarified the problem, but that they also had an outcome in mind, a proposed solution, and had already done what they could to tackle the problem. It ensured that they were focused on finding a solution and not just there to present a problem. It reminded them to take ownership of finding a solution, rather than just pass the problem on to him. And when the word spread and people knew to expect these questions, they were often pretty clear of exactly what they needed from the dean by the time they arrived at his office – whether it was his authorisation, influence, perspective, backing or his budget.

It can be quite cathartic to be on the receiving end of these kinds of questions, too. I remember calling Graham for a second opinion on an article I had written for a high-profile publication, and he asked me directly: 'What do you really need from me here? Do you need my opinion as CEO on how this piece reflects on the company? Or are you just having an insecure author moment?' The question made me laugh out loud. He was spot on: I was, indeed, having an insecure author moment. What I really needed was just a voice of reassurance. In a moment where I didn't trust my own judgement, I needed someone who knew me well, and who knows my writing well, to tell me what I needed to hear: 'Stop worrying. Trust yourself. It will be fine.' And, indeed, it was.

Do you have this on your radar?

'Rachel, are you going to be updating the brochure?'

'Yes, Dave, it's on my long list of things to do but I need to XYZ first.'

'Ok, I just wanted to know if it was on your radar.'

Not everything that arrives in your inbox is an action, but sometimes it can feel like that. When someone sends you the name of a client to contact, an idea they had for your project or a piece of information to take into account, it can sometimes feel like they've just given you another piece of work to do. Do they want you to contact them straight away? Do you need to reply? Do you need to report back to them or keep them updated?

To make life easier and avoid ambiguity, make it clear if you are requesting an action: 'Please can you update the brochure and let me know when it has been done' or, if you are leaving it with them, 'I noticed the brochure needs updating, too. Just checking you've got that on your radar as part of your branding project?'.

Dealing with mistakes

From an early age, I could tell that my children each had different ways of dealing with mistakes. One would spot a tiny mistake and want to fix it straight away. The other would try and sweep it under the carpet (sometimes literally) and try not to deal with it.

Mistakes are uncomfortable but the more we hide them, the more they tend to grow and fester. Overlooking them doesn't make them go away. If anything, it creates a breeding ground for more mistakes. But, equally, turning it into a witch hunt creates a culture of shame and blame that, naturally, makes us want to hide even more.

Graham tells me he once had a boss whose mantra about mistakes was: 'I don't care if you f*** up, as long as you own up and clear up.' What I love about this is that it tells us two things:

1. Mistakes are not the end. There is life after a mistake and what matters is what we do next.

2. It also separates the person making the mistake from the mistake itself.

The mistake is the problem. The person needs to be part of the solution. When we define ourselves by our mistakes, we can end up pouring our energies into defending, hiding or justifying our mistakes – or identifying ourselves as the failure or problem. Yes, mistakes happen and, yes, there's often a cost attached. But they're also an essential part of learning, whether that's one person learning a new job or a whole company learning a new territory.

When I was teaching my son to ride his bike, every time he fell off I knew he needed to get back on, and every time he got back on, he got a bit better. Falling off still hurt, but what choice did he have? Avoid the bike, avoid the hurt and give up altogether: failure wins. Ignore the hurt, get back on the bike, hoping he wouldn't fall off again: go into denial. The third choice was to learn to fall well: ditch the bike before you hit the ground and minimise the damage, practise on softer ground, wear protective clothing, for example. Failure sucks. It hurts, it costs, it feels bad. But if we can't avoid it or ignore it, perhaps we can learn to fail well.

What does failing well look like? Let's start with what it doesn't look like. It doesn't look like what psychologist Henry Cloud describes as the 3 Ps of learned helplessness: personal, pervasive, permanent.[3]

Imagine something bad happens: a sales call goes wrong, that product launch fails, a major client is unhappy or the date night turns into an almighty row. This is what a lot of us do in response:

1. **Make it personal** – It's my fault. I'm not good enough. I'm a failure.

2. **Make it pervasive** – It's not just this one call. It's every call. Nobody wants to buy from me. Nothing I do works. Everything sucks.

3. **Make it permanent** – It's always like this. Nothing ever works. It will always be this way. All the time.

Yes, failure hurts, but it hurts a hell of a lot more when we make it personal, pervasive and permanent. What's more, doing it this way strips away the very traits and resources we need – our belief, our courage, our vision, tenacity and hope – to recover from our mistakes and fix the problem.

How to do it instead? Instead of the 3 Ps, consider the 3 Cs: clarity, control, connection.

1. **Clarity.** Well, Henry Cloud calls it Log and Dispute, but I like alliteration so I'm calling it clarity. Clarity about what happened, what that means, and clarity about who you are. Log everything you find yourself thinking about the event itself and what that means. Log the personal, pervasive and permanent, and challenge those assumptions. For example:

   - One person didn't like what you did. What was it they didn't like exactly? What can you do about that? What do you want to do about that? Is it a failing by their measure or yours?
   - One conversation went wrong. What actually happened? What words were said in what way? What impact did they have? What else was going on at the time?
   - That was a stupid mistake; I'm so stupid I can't even get that right. Was it a stupid mistake or a simple mistake? How did it happen? What else was going on at the same time? What simple solution could you put in place to check for these simple mistakes in the future?

2. **Control.** Learned helplessness starts when something happens outside of your control. The way to counter this is to recognise where you can take control. Just as we looked at the circles of influence and concern in Chapter 2, make sure you focus your energy on what you can control or influence, rather than what you can't.

   Looking at a mistake:

   - What factors were at play that led to that mistake?
   - What could you have controlled? What was beyond your control?
   - What can you do now to fix things?
   - What can you do differently next time?
   - How can you increase your response-ability in the future?

3. **Connection.**

   > **'The human brain survives on three things: oxygen, glucose and relationships.'**
   >
   > HENRY CLOUD

When we connect with others, our perspectives change. We find new solutions to old problems and new strength to fight ongoing battles.

Falling off a bike hurts, yes, but it's far more painful if you have to do it on your own. Having support, accountability, encouragement, someone to cheer you on, help you back up, empathise with your pain and rally you back on the bike – that makes the biggest difference.

But it has to be the right people. Falling off a bike in front of someone who just laughs, criticises, belittles or blames you would be worse than doing it on your own. As social researcher Brene Brown, author of *Daring Greatly*, helpfully defines, 'Feedback is sitting on the same side of the table and looking at the issue together.' Not sitting opposite someone with the problem between you. How could you change how you look at mistakes differently? By seeking true feedback. Asking someone to sit at the same side of the table as you to help you to own up and clear up.

How can you change how your team responds to mistakes?

By creating a safe environment to own up. By being more interested in understanding mistakes and finding solutions than apportioning blame. And by giving feedback in a way that says it's not about me against you. You're not the problem. Your mistake/behaviour/obstacle is.

Let's look at that together.

Firefighting like the pros

Sometimes things don't go to plan. Sometimes plans change. Sometimes we have to fight fires. We often associate firefighting with panic, chaos, running around like a headless chicken. But how do the professionals fight fires?

- **With calm and focus.** Firefighters assess the situation and deal with it. They know that panic impairs their ability to make the right decisions, so they ensure that their heads are in the right place to respond quickly and effectively.

- **As a team.** Firefighters rarely go and tackle fires by themselves. They recognise that working as part of a team means that they cover each other's backs and blind spots, provide reinforcement and extra capacity to lighten the load. Communication is vital to ensure everyone is working together in the same direction and helping, rather than hindering. Who is part of your team? Who can give you that extra perspective, sanity check or extra hand? What happens when a crisis hits? Do you shut everyone out? Does all your team run around doing their own thing? Or do you pull together to put out the fire?

- **With a plan.** Firefighters always have a plan. They spend time away from the fires working out how best to tackle fires. They do the thinking upfront so that, in the heat of the moment, they already know exactly what they need to do and can spring into action straight away. How much space do you make in your week to clarify your strategy and plans?

- **With protection.** They take care of themselves. They make sure they are fit to fight fires. They take care to ensure they don't compromise their ability to continue fighting fires by putting themselves at risk in one fire.

- **With prevention.** A large part of a firefighter's job is spent educating people and raising awareness to prevent fires. The more fires they can prevent, the fewer fires they have to fight and, of course, the lower the cost in lives (and resources).

- **With capacity.** Firefighters always take capacity really seriously. Think about it, at any given time you wouldn't want the entire fireforce out fighting fires because who's going to deal with the next one? Firefighters make sure they always have the capacity to respond – even if they can't predict when the next fire is going to be. How much margin do you give yourself?

The importance of margin

Most of us tend to fill our calendars to the brim, trying to figure out how to squeeze another five-minute job in between those two meetings. We think that makes us efficient.

I have come to realise that I'm a filler, by nature. Give me time and my natural instinct is to fit something in. Give me space and I see boundless opportunities. I like to be productive, get lots done, lead a rich and varied life, work and play, have my cake and eat it. If you're like me, you will know that amazing feeling when it all comes together and works like a dream and the nightmare it is when it falls apart. And, let's face it, when we stack the bricks up high, it doesn't take much to topple the tower – a snow day, a sick day, a bad night, an unexpected phone call, a family emergency, a burst pipe, broadband outage, car trouble or an explosive nappy. And, sometimes, it's entirely down to me, fitting in that phone call or errand when I'm running 10 minutes early, forgetting that nothing ever takes 5 minutes and ending up 20 minutes late.

Counter-intuitively, the most powerful productivity tool we can have in our arsenal is margin.

Margin is the space between our load and our limits. It's having time beyond what is necessary. It's blank space in the diary that gives us time to deal with the work that overspills, the unexpected glitches and the emergency firefighting. It's breathing space that gives us time to change our minds, think, grow, laugh and play and the choice to stop. Like air in a pillow, the value of space is, in itself, immaterial, but it plays a vital role between what is solid, allowing for movement and comfort and absorbing impact.

Having margin means that when that lightning bolt of creative genius hits, we can go with it wholeheartedly and discover what we could never have planned for. It gives us the freedom to be pleasantly interrupted by a cuddle, a smile, an unexpected call or the jingle of an ice-cream van. And it gives us the capacity to be responsive to a cry for help, to receive an unexpected blessing, to be captivated by a perfect sunset or a child's first step, and to be spontaneous when we wake up to snow.

> 'So many people are being robbed from a life of meaning, not because they are not committed but because they are over-committed.'
>
> CRAIG GROESCHEL[4]

Spare capacity can mean the world. Spare capacity can change the world. What if we had the capacity to stop for just five minutes a day to help someone out: to hold the door, give directions, stop and smile or tell someone to take their time? Or, when someone turns up unexpectedly, to say 'pull up a chair and join us', to wait with the child who's just fallen off her scooter until her mum catches up or to help the old man with rickety knees get his bags down the stairs.

The thing about margin is we all love the idea. But, in reality, in a world where we are already stretched, it seems really, really hard to do! The trick is to start small. Here are some ideas:

- Build an extra hour or day into your deadline.

- Leave the office 10 minutes early to reach that appointment.

- Book in a 30-minute slot for a 20-minute meeting (make sure everyone is aware it's a 20-minute meeting).

- Take one thing off today's to-do list and don't replace it.

- Say 'no' to one meeting or one extra request this week.

- Ask for that file a day earlier than you need it.

- Give yourself a lunch break and, when you take it, leave the phone at your desk.

- Give yourself an extra 10 minutes on top of travel time in between your meetings, so you can gather your thoughts, capture your actions, etc.

- Set your 'out of office' autoreply to tell people you return from holiday one day later than you actually come back, so you can catch up with yourself before everyone wants a piece of you. (Let the people who can see you in your office know that's what you're doing – or work from home).

- ....

- ....

Let others do what they can do

Delegate: to entrust (a task or responsibility) to another person.

Part of creating margin is letting others do what they can do, so you can do what only you can do. Yes, they might do it more slowly, or badly to begin with. Yes, it will take time to get them up to speed – so, initially, it may slow you down, too. And, no, they probably won't do it the same way as you. To delegate is to entrust; to let go of the fine control and trust someone else to get the job done. The goal is to stop being the bottleneck.

The easiest things to delegate are simple tasks and well-documented processes – worker-mode tasks, where you have already defined the parameters of the job and it's just up to someone else to execute it. What's harder is where decisions are involved but, even then, you can still build in margin, for example:

> *'Many thanks for your email. I have cc'd in one of our Productivity Ninjas, Grace, who would be delighted to run through the options for you and your team. She will be in touch as soon as she is free to help you (please bear in mind that she may be delivering a workshop at the moment, though, so may not be able to respond today).'*

Or, for Richard Tubb, an IT business consultant who occasionally gets interview requests from people in far-flung time zones that fall outside of his normal working hours, instead of asking his PA to check with him each time (and making himself the bottleneck), I suggested giving his PA the authorisation to pencil in appointments and set expectations accordingly:

> *'Richard doesn't normally have appointments on those days/at those times, but he will make an exception to accommodate your time zone. Let me pencil you in and confirm once I have checked with him/let you know if that is a problem.'*

What about managing up?

> *'I'm pretty good at organising myself, but I don't know what to do with my boss!'*

> *'I think I'm on track, then wham – my boss comes out of a meeting and it's all change again!'*

> *'Everything's urgent and last-minute. How can I plan ahead if my boss doesn't?'*

Let's face it: sometimes the chaos does come from the top. And, for some of us, we've been that person too. But it's not enough simply to hand over the reins and put our boss in charge of our workload. The truth is we are all boss and worker, whatever level of the organisation we are in. Whether you run your own company, are the CEO of a large organisation, or an entry-level assistant just starting out, most of us work in roles where our job is as much about deciding what to work on, what not to work on, defining the work, what 'job done' looks like, what success looks like (boss mode) as it is how to go about it and get the job done (worker mode). And, to do that well, we need to manage our relationship with those who give us work as well as those we work with.

Jenny was at her wits' end with her boss. He would email her ideas off the top of his head, usually with a super-tight deadline, she would work hard to deliver what she thought he wanted, only to have him redo everything or change his mind about what he wanted. She was someone who prided herself on getting things right, but it felt like however hard she tried, it was never right with him. In fact, often she would deliver something that worked fine but, by the time he tweaked and fiddled with it, he would hand it back to her broken. She started questioning herself, her competence and capability and, almost like a self-fulfilling prophecy, she started making mistakes in other areas of her work, too.

So how do you deal with a seagull boss (someone who flies in, dumps on you, then flies off again) or an overenthusiastic Tigger who doesn't realise the havoc he causes?

Understand what's happening behind the scenes

When we personalise the situation, we start to think that it's either all our fault, like Jenny did, or all their fault: he doesn't care, she's failing to communicate or, even, they are doing it on purpose.

Take a step back and look at the wider picture. What's going on in the wider world? Are you in a season of rapid change? Is your boss reacting to new mandates as much as you are? Do they have a 'seagull boss' firing surprises at them every day? Are they reacting to a new industry climate or a demanding customer? Are they suffering from new-parent sleep deprivation? Or is it part of their personality? Do they naturally tend to think much more in the moment? Are they firing ideas at you at the point where they are forming, rather than when they're fully formed?

Why this is good for you: you stop winding yourself up.

Why this is good for your boss: you understand what's motivating them or winding them up.

Result: you move from 'why are you doing this to me?' to 'what's going on and how can I help?'.

Understand what they want from you

Are they clear about what they want from you or are they inviting your input in defining the work? Do they have the bare bones of an idea they want you to add flesh to? Do they have an idea they want you to expand by yourself or help them explore? Are they saying 'build this end-product ready to deliver to the client' or 'can you put something together along these lines to see what it might look like' or, even, 'hey, I've got a new idea, can you help me figure out if it's got legs?'.

Knowing what they want will help you to avoid putting in hours of fine detail when all that's needed is an overview, or avoid delivering a quick and dirty one-pager when they actually want a 50-page report.

Jenny thought her boss wanted her to deliver the final product, so every time he changed his mind she felt like she was having to redo work. In fact as an ideas person, her boss was just asking her to put each stage of his idea into action, so each iteration was actually progress because it helped him to get one step closer to the final goal.

Why this is good for you: you don't have to guess – you know exactly what's being asked of you.

Why this is good for your boss: they get what they want.

Result: you don't waste time second-guessing and running in opposite directions.

Understand their communication style – and yours

If they have a tendency to think out loud, what they say at the beginning may not be the decision they end up with at the end. Make sure you listen to the idea as it unfolds and check that you have understood the final decision of what they want you to do. Ask if you can email them with a summary of your understanding of what has been agreed – so that you're both clear about what you're working towards and what your next actions will be.

If you need more time to process what's been said, say that you would like to digest this further and ask if you can come back to them within a particular timeframe with any questions – or even before you make a decision. If you need a checkpoint halfway through, schedule that in at the beginning: 'Let me put some rough ideas together and send them over. Can we check in on Wednesday to make sure I'm on the right track?'.

Why this is good for you: you don't have to do all your thinking on the spot.

Why this is good for your boss: they're free to communicate in their own style, and so are you.

Result: fewer misunderstandings, better communication.

Pre-empt, don't mind read

If your boss has a habit of asking for things at the last minute, the more you know about their projects and deadlines, the more you can pre-empt and call attention to things that might require your input ahead of time:

'You're meeting with the client next week. Is there anything you'll be needing from me before then?'

'The deadline for submission is at the end of the month. Let me get a draft to you by 15th, then we can meet on 17th to review and agree any changes.'

'Who else is involved in this project? Do we need to get their input on this, too?'

'Have you considered...'?

Why this is good for you: you get to plan ahead with fewer surprises.

Why this is good for your boss: they get to plan ahead with fewer surprises!

Result: more proactive, less reactive working on both sides.

Use an umbrella

Ok, sometimes, when it comes pouring down, you do need an umbrella! If you find yourself on the receiving end of a barrage of emails, with enthusiastic new ideas, hot-off-the-press requests or a furious rant, can you defer the decision and buy some cooling-off time?

'That's a great idea. Let me come back to you.'

'Let me get this project out of the door, then I'll be able to give this my full attention.'

'Lots of great ideas here. Best to talk them over. How about Friday?'

'I'll discuss this with...'

'Let me think this over.'

'Let's talk in the morning.'

Why this is good for you: you create breathing room to respond rather than react.

Why this is good for your boss: they know that their idea or issue has been acknowledged and is in hand.

Result: you respond to the core of the issue with your best answers rather than react to the noise surrounding it.

Offer alternatives

It can be hard to say 'no' outright to your boss. But if what they're asking for is not going to work, or is likely to be costly, it's up to you to communicate that.

'I can give you the quick-and-dirty version today or the fully polished version next Thursday. Which would you prefer?'

'I can get this to you by close of play tomorrow, if I put Project X on the back burner. That means we'll have to push back the launch to May. What do you want to do?'

'The earliest I can get this to you is Wednesday. What you can use in the meantime is...'

'What about...?'

'This is what I can do...'

Why this is good for you: you can negotiate what works best for you.

Why this is good for your boss: your perspective gives them added clarity of what's doable and what the impact is.

Result: more of the right things get done (and there's a common understanding of what those right things are).

Building trust

'Trust lies at the heart of a functioning, cohesive team. Without it, team-work is all but impossible,' writes Patrick Lencioni in his book *The Five Dysfunctions of Team*. 'Teams that lack trust waste inordinate amounts of time and energy managing their behaviours and interactions within the group. They tend to dread team meetings, and are reluctant to take risks in asking for or offering assistance to others.'

Without trust, we can end up doubling up on the work: running through the figures ourselves to make sure they've done it; checking and triple-checking and worrying in between; it takes up extra space in our heads when we can't just leave it with someone. We might even decide that it's not worth the worry and that it's easier to do it ourselves. At least we know it's done and done properly then.

We may hold back from saying what we really mean. If we don't trust someone to have our best interests at heart, we're likely to think a lot more over how we say things and what we reveal. We might be more defensive in our communication, perceive or create conflict where there was none to begin with and end up having more conversations in our head instead of directly with each other. We can spend time justifying or proving our point of view, rather than focusing on moving actions and

outcomes forward, and we can feel the need to fix how we feel, rather than address the problem at hand. We can find ourselves dancing around each other, covering our backs, avoiding conflict, hiding mistakes, protecting ourselves and valuing impression management over productivity.

To build trust, we need to be able to say what we need, admit when we don't know, shout when we are in over our heads and confess when we've messed up. In other words, we need to be vulnerable and open with our mistakes, our weaknesses, our shortcomings and requests for help – and to know that it's safe to do so.

'It's only when team members are truly comfortable being exposed to one another that they begin to act without concern for protecting themselves. As a result, they can focus their energy and attention completely on the job at hand, rather than on being strategically disingenuous or political with one another.'

Over to you

What real-world tactics will you use to make a difference to the way that you work with those around you?

What I could use as a 'do not disturb' signal:

....

Where I can go to practise stealth and camouflage:

....

Who needs to know? How will I communicate this?

....

People I work closely with that I can start using an agenda for:

....

One thing I can suggest to my team/boss/co-workers to improve the way we keep each other updated:

....

One thing I will do to create more margin this week:

....

One way I can enable or encourage my team to create more margin:

....

How well do I manage up? One thing I can do to improve the way I manage my boss/clients/key stakeholders:

....

....

....

....

....

Conversations to have with my team

What do we need to let go of?

....

....

....

What's hampering our productivity at the moment? How much of this are we creating, contributing towards or reinforcing?

....

....

....

What do you want and what do you need from me?

....

....

....

Do we have a safe environment to be vulnerable and open with our mistakes, our weaknesses, our shortcomings and requests for help?

....

....

....

What would help to build more trust?

....

....

....

....

Chapter 6

Tough love: setting boundaries and saying no

Y ou know you can't be everything to everyone, right? But, even when you know, it's still hard to put it into practice. Here are some practical ways of setting healthy boundaries and expectations, managing your availability and saying no with grace and confidence.

Why we struggle to define boundaries

We struggle to define boundaries because we think they are about keeping people out. We don't want to be rude, ungenerous or unwelcoming. We don't want to turn clients away or put people off. We don't want to offend or upset. We fear putting our jobs or our relationships on the line, because we don't want to push people away:

'I don't want to be too specialist because I don't want to put people off.'

'I don't want to say no because I don't want to be rude or unhelpful.'

'I don't want to tick off my boss'

'We can't ignore our customers!'

But boundaries are actually more about valuing what's inside, than keeping people out. The most helpful definition I have come across is in Danny Silk's parenting book, *Loving Our Kids On Purpose:*

> **'Boundaries communicate value for what is inside of those boundaries. If you have several junk cars out in a field, it's called an *eyesore*. If you put a fence around those cars, then you have a *wrecking yard*. And if you put a building around those cars, you have a *garage*. With each increase of limits you increase the value of what is inside. When you raise the level of what you require before you will allow access, you increase the value of what you have. To all who are near, we send a clear message about the level of value we have for ourselves by the way we establish boundaries.'**
>
> **DANNY SILK[1]**

To have boundaries you have to value yourself. What are you really saying when you always have time for others and not yourself? What are you saying about the value of your personal time, when you work through the night and into the weekend? Or the value of your family time when your emails join you at the dinner table? What are you saying about the value of your services if you constantly undercharge or give them away for free, or the value of your health or sanity if you're regularly sacrificing sleep in order not to let anyone else down?

How valuable is your time and attention? How valuable is your contribution? How valuable are you? Or your team? Or your family?

Boundaries are not about who or what we keep out. They exist to honour what we value.

What happens when you don't set boundaries

Initially, in the short term, it might just be an inconvenience – an extra hour here, an extra commitment there, cancelling one of your own plans or being out of pocket once. But when it keeps happening, an inconvenience becomes a toleration, and the longer you tolerate something the more of a toll it takes and the more established it becomes.

Tim's always in the office early.

Sarah's always the last one to leave.

Kate can always pick up the pieces.

Mum's never home.

Dad's always on his phone.

An exception becomes the norm and reluctance becomes resentment. Somewhere along the line, something we chose to let happen becomes something that happens to us. We feel powerless and we lose ourselves in the process.

No one else can set our boundaries for us. It's up to us to define what we value and how much we value it. It's up to us to establish the rules of engagement and to set expectations. Just like the walls of a house provide definition, support and security, we find that when we do set boundaries they actually strengthen and enhance our relationships, as well as our productivity.

What one boundary can you put in place this week that would make a significant difference to you?

What happens when you try and please everybody

So you think you want to please everybody? Here is what happens:

When you're afraid to turn down an opportunity

'Ahrrrghhhh! Why did I take this project on? Why, why whyyyyyy? Grrrrrrrrrrrrrrrrrrrr! This project may be stable and lucrative but it's a massive pain in the bum! Is it wine time yet?!'

The curse of the capable is that there are lots of things we can do even if it's not what we do best, what we enjoy doing best, or what gets the best out of us. It's a classic case for most new (and some not-so-new) businesses – but it happens just as much in employment, too: the extra project you're asked to be involved in because you've some expertise or experience in that area; the client who's not ideal or the jobs you take on 'just to tide you over'; the tasks that need doing that may not be your field of expertise but, nevertheless, need to be done.

We've all done it and, when it enables you to do what you love and move forward in the right direction, it can have its place. Being flexible and resourceful and willing to do the hard things is both necessary and noble. But operating outside of your strengths zaps you and can easily take over your time, energy and headspace, leaving you with no capacity or strength for what you really want to do, what you do best and what energises you. When you settle for what you can do, too often, it can leave you feeling resentful, frustrated, unfulfilled or drained.

When you shy away from saying what you mean

When you ask your other half if they're sure they wouldn't prefer a takeaway (because you're really tired and can't be bothered to make dinner) and they tell you they would choose your cooking over a takeaway any day.

When you ask someone if they know of anyone who could help you do something, when really you want them to offer, and they don't get the hint.

When you ask a colleague, 'How was the traffic this morning? Is everything ok?', then accept a vague answer that leaves you none the wiser why they're often 15–30 minutes late for key meetings.

When someone who's come into your office for a chat outstays their welcome and you keep looking at your screen, but they don't seem to be getting the hint.

Sometimes, we find it hard to say what we really mean, so we drop hints and might even try to sell a more attractive alternative instead of asking for what we really need. The problem with this is it involves mind reading and can often leave us feeling frustrated or even resentful.

When you don't want to hurt someone's feelings

What happens when you have to deliver bad news, give critical feedback to one of your team or explain to a client that what they want can't be done?

The phrase 'don't shoot the messenger' comes to mind, but where you are invested in the outcome a hit-and-run strategy might not be that helpful. For those of us who do like to please people and avoid upsetting others, there's also a danger of taking too much responsibility.

Every communication has three parts – the message, how it's delivered and how it's received. Your responsibility only goes as far as crafting and delivering the message – which, of course, you can adapt to be as helpful as possible – but, ultimately, the other person has a choice in how they receive it. Your job is to deliver the message well. If you make yourself responsible for their happiness, you're taking responsibility that doesn't belong to you.

When you say yes because you hate saying no

Listen, if you love to be generous, that's a good thing! But there's a difference between generosity and being a doormat. Being generous has to come from a place of 'I'd love to' rather than 'I have to'. When you say yes too often, when really you want to say no, this will lead to resentment.

Generosity has been described as a fruit of the spirit. Fruit nourishes and replenishes you. If you're feeling drained by giving too much, giving from a place of empty because you 'can't say no', that's not generosity, that's something else. Generosity has to be a choice from the heart, not from a place of obligation, duty, guilt or expectation.

But here's what happens when you stop trying to please everybody: you let go of the stuff that's not right for you – and clear space for what is

A good friend invited me to join her on a project recently. I love her work and her style and would relish the opportunity to work with her. But the role was not right for me at that time. After much deliberation, I realised the only reason I hadn't said no straight away was because I didn't want to say no to her. It turns out that she had picked up that my heart wasn't in it and had already found someone else. As she put it, 'I can't really have someone who doesn't want to be there.' You see, if an opportunity's not right for you, you're not right for it either. I wouldn't have done it any justice if I had said yes.

Similarly, I had a journalist request a while ago, asking if I would comment on seasonal marketing for small businesses. She had picked up on a guest post on my blog so, instead of saying yes and trying to fit myself into that space, I put her in touch with the person who wrote that blog post, who is an expert in that area. As a result, I didn't spend hours figuring out what I would say, worrying about an interview that had nothing to do with my strengths and expertise, and I had so much more mental clarity to focus on what was right for me and my business instead.

Over the years, I've found that every time I say no to an opportunity that's not right for me, a better opportunity comes along.

You stop mind reading and ask for what you need

'I'm really tired tonight, love. Shall I get a takeaway or do you want to cook?'

'I need some help with this project – do you have capacity to take on an extra client right now?'

'Is there any reason why you're often 15–30 minutes late for key meetings?'

'I need to dive into this report now, but I'm free at lunchtime if you need some help figuring that one out.'

When you ask for what you need, and ask others what they need, you can come up with a solution together. No more mind reading!

You honour who you are – and let others do the same

When you stop trying to be all things to all people, you do your best, most impactful and most satisfying work. You give your best from a place of plenty and find you have so much more to give. Not only that, you give others the opportunity to step up and give their best too.

Be yourself. When you honour who you are – and who you're not – you also honour and accept others for who they are.

Leading those you serve

I have a local taxi company that's very reliable. Their prices are consistent, their drivers are always on time and they don't dawdle to rack up the meter. By all accounts they offer excellent service, until something goes wrong. I once ordered a taxi to pick me up from the train station at 11:30 pm. The train had already been delayed when I called, so I explained that I hoped to be at the station for that time. As it happened, I was delayed by a further 10 minutes. By the time I arrived at the station, there was no taxi in sight. I called the company.

'Well, you booked it for 11:30. When you didn't show, the driver left.'

'Ok, but my train was delayed.'

'You could have called us.'

'True, but the signal on the train isn't great – plus, I already told you it was running late.'

'We had no way of knowing if you were coming. The driver can't afford to wait around for no shows.'

'You knew I was on a train. There's not much of a chance I'm not going to show, is there?'

'Well, I can send him back.'

'How long will that be?'

'10 minutes.'

'Never mind, I can see there's a taxi at the rank. I'll take that instead.'

'So, you're saying you don't want a taxi now?'

'Yes.'

'Fine.' Hangs up.

Well, that was a pretty poor outcome for both of us. The driver and the company lost out on a fare. As the customer, I felt let down. Nobody wins.

What is interesting about this conversation is that nothing the taxi company did was wrong, as such. But the way in which they did it left them out of pocket and the customer feeling let down. They were enforcing boundaries that were pretty fair, but hadn't been communicated. And, when questioned, their response was defensive, which of course got my back up too. With hindsight (which is a wonderful thing), here's what they could have done differently:

- **Set clear expectations about delays:** 'Our drivers will wait for five minutes max. If you're delayed longer than that, you need to let us know.'

- **Acknowledge the dilemma:** 'I'm sorry about that. Our drivers can only wait for five minutes, as we often get no shows. What I can do is send someone back. They'll be there in 10 minutes. Would you like me to do that?'

- **Offer a better solution for the future:** 'Listen. Next time, give us a call when you're 10 minutes away. That way we'll be able to get a taxi to you by the time you arrive and there's less chance of your train being delayed at that point.'

Setting the boundary upfront would have also prompted me to offer to pay for waiting time, which I would have been happy to do (I don't want the driver to be out of pocket, but I'd rather not be a lone female hanging around a train station at that time of night). They could have said yes or no to that, but at least I would know exactly what to expect.

On another occasion with the same company, a taxi turned up at my house to take me to the airport, but didn't knock on the door. When the time had passed, I called the company. 'Well, they waited outside, but you didn't come out', they said. I wasn't told I had to look out (maybe I missed taxi etiquette school?). Apparently, they saw that the curtains were closed and took that as a sign that no one was at home. Of course, the curtains were closed because I was about to go to the airport.

Since then, it turns out that they actually have a ring-back service – two rings on your number when the taxi arrives. But I only found that out when I specifically asked: 'Do I need to look out for them or will they knock?' I have resigned myself to the fact that, with this company, I have to take the lead in any conversation if I want to know where I stand. This is a shame, as if they had taken the lead in setting expectations, they would have far more delighted customers and fewer missed fares.

How often do you feel aggrieved when your boundaries are crossed? How clearly have you communicated them? How much have you assumed that they will know? How much do you lead your customer and set their expectations or do you leave it up to them to second-guess and mind read?

Often, we think that serving means to let someone else take the lead and to respond or react as appropriate, whether that's customer service, serving our community, our boss or our family members. We ask them what they want and we endeavour to give it to them. When what they want crosses a line of possibility or appropriateness – in our minds – we find ourselves in conflict.

But that places a huge amount of responsibility on the person we're serving: to know what's possible; to know what's appropriate. If you walked into a restaurant of a certain calibre, you would expect the waiter to guide you to a table, give you a menu, tell you if anything is not available that day, maybe give you some recommendations or specials of the day and ask you what you'd like to drink. Yes, if you asked for a different table or an alternative side dish they would also respond to that. But if they simply said, 'What do you want?' when you arrived, that would be pretty hard work for you as the customer, let alone the waiter and the chef!

Sometimes we serve best when we take the lead, when we define what we have to offer and how we work best, when we do the hard work of working out the best way of meeting our customers' needs, when we set clear expectations up front and guide the customer through the experience:

- I serve my children when I offer them a balanced meal – rather than asking them what they want (chocolate, chocolate and more chocolate).

- I serve my clients when I let them know my working hours and availability.

- I serve my colleagues when I tell them I can give my best answer on Friday rather than a rushed and hurried one now.

- I serve my church when I tell them that I don't have the capacity to give that project the attention it deserves.

- I serve my husband when I ask for help with the laundry rather than huff and puff with resentment that I have to do everything myself.

How can you serve your people better, by taking a lead, defining boundaries and setting clear expectations?

How you work best

If you're a designer who works best when you get a feel for your client's passion, style and personality – and are much more inspired by an intimate chat over coffee than a detailed project brief – then tell them that. If, on the other hand, you need a structured brief to work from and your client is notoriously bad at providing detail, then acknowledge that there's a translation job to be done first:

'I'm going to email you with a summary of what we've agreed. What I'd like you to do is to reply and confirm I've captured everything accurately before I start working on it.'

If you prefer to digest things internally and give your best input when you've had time to think, ask your clients to email you their ideas or an agenda before the meeting, so you can be prepared. Let them know that's how you work best. If they surprise you with an idea, don't be flustered, accept it with the enthusiasm it was offered and buy yourself time by saying, 'Let me think on that and come back to you'.

On the other hand, if you think best on your feet and in conversation, then reply to the email with, 'Let's talk about this. I'd like to understand a bit more about... How's Friday for you?'.

If you like to have the whole picture before you begin, then ask for it. Explain that once you know what you're doing, you will go away, get it done and come back to them with everything complete. If, on the other hand, you prefer a step-by-step approach and prefer to get feedback along the way, agree some checkpoints in advance.

If you're holding dates for someone, how long will you hold them for? I once spent a week holding one opportunity at bay while I checked if someone else still wanted a date they had asked me to hold a few weeks ago. I couldn't get hold of them in the end and had to release the date. It was time-consuming and frustrating for me and I worried about disappointing the first client. Graham reminded me that for this reason we have a policy of holding dates for one week and that when we're clear about this upfront, clients benefit from the certainty of having their dates on hold for a week and know that, if they take longer than a week, those dates will get released and may be booked by someone else.

How do you work best? How often will you check in? What's the best way to keep in touch in between meetings? What if things change? Addressing some of these questions upfront not only makes life easier for you, but also gives others more certainty in dealing with you.

Here's what happens next

One of the confirmation emails I love to get (yes, I'm probably a bit strange like that) comes from MOO (moo.com), the company that prints my business cards:

HELLO GRACE

I'm Little MOO – the bit of software that will be managing your order with **moo.com**. It will shortly be sent to Big MOO, our print machine who will print it for you in the next few days. I'll let you know when it's done and on its way to you.

If you've imported your images to MOO from another site, please make sure you don't remove or change the photos you've chosen from that site until this order has been printed, or some pictures may come out blank.

(If you've uploaded them directly to MOO, then there's no need to worry.)

You can track and manage your order from the accounts section at:

https://secure.moo.com/account

Estimated Arrival Date: Wed 10 Dec 2014

Remember, I'm just a bit of software.

So, if you have any questions regarding your order please first read our Frequently Asked Questions at:

http://www.moo.com/help/faq/

and if you're still not sure, contact Customer Service (who are real people):

By Email/Online Chat:

http://www.moo.com/help/contact-us.html

By Phone:

UK: +44(0) 207 392 2780 – 8.30am–5.30pm BST Mon-Fri (excl. public holidays); USA: 3.30am–9.00pm EDT

(Currently, our team can only handle calls in English and the call may be recorded for future training and improvement to the service – we thought you'd like to know.)

Thanks,

Little MOO, Print Robot

This answers questions that I have right now (What happens next? Anything I need to do right now?), questions I might have later (What if I need to talk to someone?) and even sets my expectations in case I was expecting to be able to talk to them in French or on a Sunday. Most of all, I love it because it's friendly and it's positive. It doesn't tell me that they're unavailable at the weekend or that they don't speak any other languages, it tells me when they **are** available and what they **can** handle. It also doesn't leave me to dig for contact details – it gives me a first port of call (FAQs) and an alternative (real people). And as it happens, MOO now does have a range of languages spoken in their Customer Service team.

'What happens next?' is a question that your clients/colleagues/boss might have. If you can take a lead on this, you give them clarity and save yourself some potential distractions when your focus is elsewhere.

How available are you?

Do you have email on 24/7? Does your phone buzz when someone tweets you? Do you wake up to that familiar red light flashing on your BlackBerry? What about the times when you're in a meeting? With a client? On the phone? When you're travelling, driving, at a conference or attending training? When you're off work? On holiday, with your kids, on a date, in the bath or asleep?

Whether you like it or not, there will be times when you're not available to answer emails – and, probably, arguably, plenty more times when you could do with being less available. Yes, there's often an expectation that an email requires a quick, or even instant, response. Yes, some industries and organisational cultures actively perpetuate this expectation. But I wonder how much of that expectation do we set ourselves?

Here are some examples of how you can actively manage expectations.

Email signatures

Paula, our Client Happiness and Logistics Manager, has this on her email signature:

'Please note we run a "4 Day Working Week" here at Think Productive, so I am out of the office most Fridays. If your issue is urgent, please call the office line below.'

And Matthew, our London Ninja has this:

*** I check emails once a day. If your matter is urgent, please call me. I am unavailable by phone and email on Fridays.***

I have also seen this work well with job-share and part-time workers, as well as people whose job involves travel, days in meetings or between different office locations. Being upfront about your availability means people know when they can get hold of you. It also means that they can pre-plan. If there's something you need from Paula or Matthew before the end of the week, ask them before the end of Thursday.

Email autoresponders

If your role requires you to dive deep with focused attention as well as being responsive to customers, you could take your inspiration from this accountant's email autoresponse:

'Thank you for your email. I am likely to be in a meeting or immersed in a client's work. So that I can give them my undivided attention and focus, this inbox is checked once a day. If you need me more urgently than this, please

text or leave a voicemail on my mobile xxxxx and I shall respond to you as soon as I am free.'

Or, for a more humorous approach, this is one recruitment consultant's email autoresponse:

'Thank you for your email.

Those that know me well will realise that the remnants of childhood hyperactivity mean that I can be distracted by the slightest thi...ooohhhh, look, a chicken!

To be more effective, and ultimately serve you better, I am only accessing emails at 12.00 pm and 4.00 pm daily. If your issue is urgent and requires my immediate attention then please call me.

Thank you for your cooperation.'

Often, when we send an email all we want to know is that it's in hand and when we'll get a reply – instead of wondering if/when we need to chase. Knowing with confidence that someone will get back to me within 24 hours allows me to park it on my waiting list and forget about it for the next 24 hours, rather than play a lottery of wondering if it will be a superfast 2-minute response or whether it will take weeks of chasing. And, of course, offering an alternative for emergencies covers the more urgent requests – which are usually far less common than we think.

Voicemail

If you call my mobile and get my voicemail, you'll hear something along the lines of:

'Thanks for calling, I'm probably with a client right now, helping them to replace stress and overwhelm with playful, productive momentum. If you'd like me to do the same for you, leave me a message and I look forward to speaking with you soon.'

I never feel guilty about letting calls go to voicemail because it usually makes people smile, doubles up as a marketing message and lets my clients know that when they are with me they get my undivided attention.

Open-office hours

My local doctors have an open surgery every morning from 8 am. If you need to see a doctor and don't have an appointment, just turn up, take a number and wait in line. A coach I know has set open-office hours when you can call for help in between sessions. If you call and the number is engaged, that means she's talking to someone else – try again in 10 minutes. If you call and get through to her, you know you'll have her undivided attention for the next 10 minutes.

My coaching clients have access to my online diary, where they can choose from available slots rather than wondering about my availability or playing email ping pong to get a date in the diary. A copywriter I know communicates her availability on her website: 'I'm now taking bookings for May', to set expectations upfront.

If you're out of the office a lot and your team find it hard to track you down, you might find it helpful all round to let people know when you're in and when you're available, to avoid being pounced on when you reappear: 'I'm travelling on Monday, in meetings Tuesday to Thursday and back in the office on Friday.'

Afternoon tea

June Dennis, Head of University of Wolverhampton Business School, schedules afternoon tea sessions for her students. She will let them know a time and place each week where she is available to answer any questions and discuss their work. She will even buy them a cup of tea.

This means her students know exactly when and where to find her, without having to hunt down her office hoping they've chosen a good time, and she gets to be less in demand during the rest of the week. It also means she can give them her full attention during that time. These are often incredibly useful conversations, where she finds out far more about her students (who's pulling all-nighters and surviving on caffeine, who's dealing with bereavement, who's struggling with home sickness) and can signpost them, advise or encourage them much more than in snatches of conversation when she's busy.

What if my boundaries have already been crossed?

It's one thing to set boundaries, but what happens if you have already allowed your boundaries to be crossed, or if you haven't been clear enough in setting them in the first place?

'People are used to me being available after-hours.'

'I've already said yes when I should have said no!'

'I said yes to fill the gap in the short term, but fast-forward nine months and there's an unspoken assumption that I'll carry on filling in the gap. I'm feeling a bit taken advantage of...'

When your boundaries have already been crossed, it can be a bit tricky to extricate yourself. If you've promised to deliver, you may not be able to pull out immediately or entirely. If you've set an expectation, it may take time to change that expectation and there may be some diplomatic retraining needed and some comfort-zone stretching for you.

Take small steps: 'I'm in the Welsh mountains this weekend so probably going to be offline. If anything comes up, just drop me an email and I'll pick it up on Monday.'

Find opportunities to revisit and redefine boundaries: We've been working together for six months now. It would be really good to review how this is working.'

'This project has really taken off – it's approaching the point where it's going to need full-time dedicated support. Let's talk about how we transition to that.'

'I've taken a deeper look and I think it's actually going to require a lot more than I initially thought. I don't have the time/expertise to do it justice right now. I'd love to support you in a different way, though. How about...'

Refer to the common outcome you share: 'Our customers need to feel valued, for sure. I'm wondering if there's a better way to achieve this. Can I run some ideas past you?'

Help others to set boundaries: 'Listen, I'm on call this weekend so you might get some emails from me – I don't need you to look at them or take any action until you're back in the office, ok?'

Ask for help: I remember one workshop where a delegate admitted that she found it really hard to say no. Her boss was in the room and said, 'Thank you for saying that. That's really good to know because I go to meetings and say yes to more work for our team because I think you have the capacity. Now that I know that's not necessarily the case, I can take that into account!'

Sometimes, when we're used to having our boundaries crossed (or not setting them in the first place), we may not be very used to asserting our own value and the validity of our boundaries. Others around you may see your value much more clearly than you can and can support you in setting and resetting your boundaries.

How to say no

Do you sometimes find yourself saying yes when you really mean to say no? Perhaps it's that really juicy opportunity or the bright, shiny, new idea that's luring you off-track? Or maybe a scary boss, a demanding client or a very important person has put you on the spot? Perhaps, like me, you're a natural helper who finds it hard to say no because you hate letting people down? Or maybe you're worried that, if you say no, they'll never ask again?

Saying no is a skill most of us have to practise. There are a rare few who find it comes naturally to them: 'No. It's just a word. What's the big deal?'. For the rest of us, there comes a point where we realise that, if we want to be able to choose what we say yes to, we need to learn how to say no comfortably, authentically, pleasantly and effectively. So here are some examples to help.

When you want to say 'not right now'

Yes, you want to help but, no, not right now. Right now, you're in the middle of drafting a delicate email, you've already got someone else breathing down your neck, a report deadline that's looming at 12 o'clock, and a meeting that starts in 10 minutes. It's not that you don't care or don't want to help, it's just really bad timing. So, if 'No, I can't right now' feels rude, abrupt or inappropriate, try saying yes on your own terms:

'Yes, I'd love to hear about that. Can we talk at 4?'

'Yes, I'm available tomorrow at 10 and at 3. Which would you prefer?'

'Yes, let's explore this properly – can we set up a meeting?'

'You know what? I'd love to give that some proper thought. Could you email me the details so I can take a closer look?'

'Yes, I'd love to help. Given my schedule, the earliest I can come back to you is... Would that work or do you want to find someone else?'

When it's a 'not this time'

It may be an event, opportunity or favour you'd normally welcome but, this time, it's not right for you – for whatever reason. I had plenty of these responses when asking for early reviewers for this book, so here are a few of my favourites:

'Sounds great. Sadly, I have to practise my ruthlessness on this one and say no. I'd love to, but I'm full up at the moment.'

'I love to read – especially your writing – but won't be able to meet the deadline.'

'The timing won't work for me this time... do please keep me in mind for future feedback.'

When you want to be supportive in a different way

Some of the best 'no' emails I have received are ones where people are genuinely encouraging:

'This sounds like a great opportunity and I'm so pleased for you. I'm fully committed with my current projects/speaking schedule/clients, but I'd love to support you by [introducing you to someone who can help/ promoting the launch/donating a raffle prize/giving you something else].'

When it's a 'thanks, but no thanks'

'Thanks so much for thinking of me. That's not really my area of expertise, but I can recommend...'

'That's very kind, but I'm going to have to decline.'

'To be honest, this isn't really my thing. You'd be much better getting x on board. Do you want me to introduce you?'

'I'm going to pass on this one – but thanks for asking!'

Instead of 'I can't', say 'I don't'

As we looked at in Chapter 3, 'I can't' signals impossibility and incapacity. It makes us feel powerless. Instead, 'I don't' sends a different signal to our brains. Whether we say it out loud or just to ourselves, it reminds us that we choose what we commit to and it feels good to honour our internal commitments:

'I don't access my emails at the weekend.'

'I don't specialise in that area.'

'I don't take calls in the evening.'

'I don't travel more than twice a month.'

'I don't take on work where I can't give my best because that doesn't serve anyone.' (Ok, that had both I don't and I can't in, but you get the idea.)

When you need to enforce boundaries

'In order to honour my existing client commitments, I only have a limited number of consultation slots available. You'll find them here...'

'I'm afraid that's only available to our workshop delegates, but I can point you to these three tips on the blog that will help you get started...'

'I'm fully committed for the next ... , but I do have availability from July onwards.'

'I've promised myself no new projects until this book's written and, now that I've told you, I have to stick to it!'

'My blogging schedule/speaking availability/advertising budget is fully committed for this month/quarter/year. Ask me again in...'

'I would love to help you out, but I already made commitments to other [co-workers, clients, etc.] to complete their projects today. It wouldn't be fair to them not to follow through on what I said I would do. I will be sure to fit this in as soon as possible. Thanks for your understanding.' (Elizabeth Grace Saunders)[2]

'Thanks for your interest in meeting with me. Unfortunately, that will not be possible for the foreseeable future. In order to honour my existing commitments, I must decline many worthy invitations like yours.' (Michael Hyatt)[3]

'Ah, that's an intriguing possibility, but I'm afraid that my own Ninja rules of life don't permit working on the weekends. Plus, I doubt the delegates would thank me/us for stealing a possible day of rest from them, given how hard the team is working right now? Hope that's ok, I was very tempted to say yes, given your keenness to get us in ASAP – but I need to stay authentic to my own Ninja principles!' (This was my Ninja colleague Lee's response to a request to run a weekend workshop for a team who couldn't find time in the week to fit in training. They did, eventually, come back to order, many months later, and the sessions were delivered in work hours, on weekdays.)

When you're totally not interested

I used to find conversations with door-to-door sales people, street fundraisers and cold callers annoying and awkward. Now I see them as an opportunity to practise saying no!

'Thanks for asking. This one's not for me, but good luck!'

'My regular giving budget is fully committed already.'

'I haven't got any advertising budget at all I'm afraid, but thanks for asking!'

'We're really not going to have a conservatory. Please don't waste your time with us.'

'Love your energy, but it's not for me, thanks!'

Incidentally, as someone who makes and follows up on sales enquiries, I love it when people do say what they mean, instead of giving me a generic 'not yet' reply, which could mean 'keep in touch' but, equally, could mean 'I wish you would stop emailing me, but I'm too polite to say so'. Knowing who genuinely wants me to follow up and who doesn't gives me clarity, which means I can stay on the ball for those who do want to continue the conversation and, equally, serve those who are no longer interested by leaving them alone!

'It's not on the cards, I'm afraid. If something changes I'll let you know. Leave it with me.'

'It's gone on the back burner, but still definitely interested. Ask me again in two months.'

'I'm still waiting on... hope to have an answer by.../check with me again next week.'

Practise

Saying no is a bit like a muscle. It can feel uncomfortable if you have not used it for a while, but the more you use it the easier it gets, and the more you realise the world really doesn't end when you do. I have also realised that I would much rather be asked and given the opportunity (and freedom) to say no, than not to be asked at all. When I feel free to say no, then others are free to ask – which means the times when I want to say yes, I can do so wholeheartedly.

Over to you

How valuable is my time and attention? How well do my boundaries reflect that?

....

....

....

Where do I feel overstretched or undervalued? Where am I prone to trying to please everybody?

....

....

....

One boundary I can put in place this week that would make a significant difference to me:

....

One area of my work or life where I can serve my people better if I take a lead in setting clear expectations:

....

One thing I can put into place to manage my availability:

....

Three ways I can practise saying no this week:

1. ....

2. ....

3. ....

Chapter 7

Being human: how your personality affects your productivity

Productivity is inherently personal. What works for one person doesn't necessarily work for someone else. Some would say the secret to productivity is to be super organised, while others say it's more about getting into the flow of your passion and creativity. Some say stop talking and get on with it, while others argue that thoughtful and consistent action wins every time.

There's probably a little bit of truth in all those statements for everyone, but we each have our own bias, preference and natural style.

The more we understand our own personality and preferences, the more we can tailor our productivity, habits and strategies to suit – rather than try and have a personality transplant. One tool I find really useful with clients is the DiSC profile.

The DiSC profile

DiSC is a behavioural assessment profile that helps you to understand yourself and the people you work with. DiSC stands for dominance, influence, steadiness and conscientiousness. It gives you insight into your working preferences and tendencies, your motivators and stressors, your needs, communication styles and how to work effectively with people who are different from you or people who are too much like you. What follows is a brief introduction to the model to give you an idea of how different behavioural styles give rise to different productivity strengths, challenges and strategies.

Meet Tim, Claudia, Sam and Kate. They are not real people but, rather, a combination of clients and colleagues I've worked with in the past, who each have different styles, needs and preferences. As you read through their examples, you might find yourself identifying strongly with one or with a blend of characters. Notice what resonates with you – and what insights you can draw out for yourself, and also notice what rings true for other people you work with – your team, your clients, your colleagues, your boss or even members of your family – and ask yourself what this might mean for how you work and relate to them.

Meet Tim

Tim is bold, ambitious and driven. He loves a challenge and is always the one to push for new horizons and stretch goals. If you want to get something done quick, Tim's your man. He will cut to the chase and have the wheels in motion quicker than you can say 'let's have a meeting'.

His colleagues love his confidence and drive. He's a force of nature: straight to the point and not afraid to speak his mind. He's a great person to have on your side, but woe betide the person who gets in his way. His single-minded focus always gets results but can be hard for others to keep up with and can, sometimes, cause collateral damage or land him in hot water.

He's a doer who doesn't have time for indecisiveness and gets bored by the mundane and routine. He hates being bogged down by red tape and protocol. His directness can sometimes come across as rude and his impatience can make him dismissive of slower or indecisive people. But if you want to get something done quickly or to confront the elephant in the room, he's your man.

If you're anything like Tim, you'll probably find that:

You enjoy: initiating change, taking risks, thinking big, being bold and taking charge. To stay motivated, make sure you have plenty of clear actions and immediate results to focus on, are being challenged by stretching goals and healthy competition and have a good dose of freedom and independence to make your own decisions.

You're drained by: too much detail, mundane and routine tasks. Watch out for procrastination here. Look for opportunities to delegate, automate, or create a challenge by turning it into a game to see how fast you can get things done.

You get frustrated by: indecisiveness and having to slow down. Avoid long-winded meetings and having nothing to do when you have to wait. Give others the opportunity to think ahead, or allow processing time afterwards. Agree timings and dates so you can park it in @waiting and get on with something else. Offer to join meetings later, when the details have been hacked out and a decision is ready to be made.

Your biggest fears: are likely to come from losing control, being taken advantage of or feeling vulnerable. Watch out for your lizard brain when you feel threatened in these areas.

Things that come naturally to you: being decisive, taking charge, casting bold vision and speaking up when nobody else will. Offer these skills to your colleagues – not everyone finds this easy!

Things to tell your colleagues:

'I need the big picture – just give me the headlines.'

'Don't worry about sugar-coating. You can get straight to the point with me.'

'I need to know why we're doing this – what does success look like here? What's the outcome?'

'Bear with me, I can be very direct. Excuse me if I come across as blunt. I don't mean to be rude.'

'I tend to move quickly and think on my feet. Let me know if I'm going too fast and you need more time to process.'

'If I've upset you, please tell me.'

Meet Claudia

Claudia is outgoing, enthusiastic and optimistic. A real people person, Claudia comes alive when she's around people – whether that's networking in a room full of strangers, collaborating on projects or having a good natter with friends.

Her colleagues love her passion and energy. A natural storyteller and networker, she can both charm and inspire audiences of all sizes, which is why she's likely to be one of the most well-connected people they know. Her enthusiasm is infectious and brings life to any meeting or party, although sometimes her tendency to gloss over detail can come across as fluffy. An eternal optimist, she likes to see possibility in every idea and tends to trust and look for the best in people, which makes her more cautious colleagues nervous.

Impulsive and creative, she prefers to go with the flow. While she's quite happy to fly by the seat of her pants, this can cause chaos for those who prefer a little more stability and preparation and earn her a reputation for being a bit flaky and last-minute. Although she wishes she was more organised, she does secretly like the buzz of a deadline. In fact, when there's no deadline in sight, she might run out of steam and be distracted by the next shiny thing before she's had a chance to follow through.

If you're anything like Claudia, you'll probably find that:

You enjoy: the buzz of new ideas, working with others, expressing yourself and being on the move. To stay motivated, look for opportunities to talk through your ideas, collaborate, focus on forward movement and express your goals as inspiring positive outcomes rather than problems or pain you want to avoid, and build in plenty of opportunity for positive external feedback.

You're drained by: too much detail, structure, systematic tasks and too much time alone – watch out for procrastination here. Seek an accountability partner, a change of scenery, or look for creative ways to spice up the boring work – and get moving. Your energy comes from being on the move so if you find yourself stuck in a rut, do something (anything) that gets you started.

You get frustrated by: critical questions and you shy away from giving unpleasant feedback – you see this as being negative. Be aware that, sometimes, other colleagues simply may have a more naturally questioning style and may not be directly attacking you or your ideas. And sometimes colleagues appreciate you being direct with them! Also look for where others are passionate – they might be more reserved or quieter in expressing it, but seeing their passion will help you to get inspired.

Your biggest fears: are likely to be around social rejection, disapproval, loss of influence and being ignored. Watch out for your lizard brain when you feel threatened in these areas.

Things that come naturally to you: socialising, networking, encouraging, brainstorming and inspiring. These are skills you enjoy using and probably find fun and energising, so let your colleagues know that you would welcome the opportunity to use them!

Things to tell your colleagues:

'Can I give you the broad idea and ask you to flesh out the detail?'

'What else do you need to know?'

'I love a good brainstorm. I'm here if you want to talk it through.'

'I think best in conversation – can we have a chat about this?'

'Am I getting carried away here? Is there anything I've missed?'

'Please feel free to nudge me in a couple of weeks, if you haven't heard from me.'

'I'd like your feedback – what do you like, what are you not so keen about and what questions do you have?'

Meet Sam

Sam is thoughtful, friendly and patient. A natural helper, Sam loves being part of a team and meeting other people's needs.

His colleagues love his calm, collaborative and supportive nature. He's a true team player, a genuine nice guy and, some would say, the glue that holds everyone together. He takes a steady, methodical and thorough approach to his work and can always be relied upon to see a job through to completion, but sometimes can frustrate others who want to move forward at a quicker pace. Not one for the limelight, he much prefers to be in the background, refining systems and making everything run smoothly, but he does appreciate genuine praise and knowing that he's making a difference.

Because he gets a lot of satisfaction from helping others, he's incredibly accommodating and will often put other people's needs above his own. He shies away from conflict so may not always speak his mind, especially if more expressive characters have the floor. He values consensus and collaboration over speed, which can sometimes lead to indecisiveness.

His natural empathy, combined with his patience, makes him a great listener and an incredibly loyal asset to the team. He's the one who remembers everyone's birthdays and always goes the extra mile to make sure a customer is totally satisfied.

If you're anything like Sam, you'll probably find that:

You enjoy: collaboration, helping people, giving support and working to a steady rhythm. To stay motivated, break big goals into steady steps, build-in routines that give you stability, seek opportunities to collaborate, develop relationships, focus on how your work supports others, ask for feedback and make sure you have a support network too.

You're drained by: conflict, too much task-focused work rather than people-focused work, having to make major decisions independently, being overstretched – watch out for procrastination and burnout here. Seek opportunities to collaborate: engage your customers or stakeholders so you can be motivated by the people that you are helping, ask for help to talk through and break down major decisions, build-in me time to make sure you're tending to your own needs.

You get frustrated by: decisions that overlook people, working in a tense or chaotic environment, being rushed and reacting to last-minute changes. Ask for thinking time to process and build in routines and rhythms to give yourself some certainty, especially if you're in a season of rapid change. Remember that chaos or conflict is not always negative or personal; give people room to rant and blow-off steam and know that, sometimes, the best teams don't always have to agree to be able to work together. If you are making a case for people to someone who is task-/results-focused, get them on board by drawing the focus back to how it affects bottom-line results.

Your biggest fears: are likely to be around loss of stability, change, loss of harmony and offending others. Watch out for your lizard brain when you feel threatened in these areas.

Things that come naturally to you: establishing routines and habits, systemising and making things methodical, breaking big goals into step-by-step actions, bringing a team together, getting people to collaborate, listening, bringing calm to chaos – you probably do all this so naturally that you don't even acknowledge it as a strength. But not everyone finds it easy, so give yourself permission to shine in these areas and take pride in your natural talents.

Things to tell your colleagues:

'This is becoming a regular thing. Shall I create a process to make everyone's life easier?'

'I'd like to process this a bit further – can I drop you a line later with some more ideas/questions?'

'I like to be prepared – can you send me an agenda so I can make sure I come with my best ideas?'

'Can we have a quick catch up next week to make sure I'm on the right track?'

'Can I send you the draft to make sure I'm on the right track?'

'How urgent is this? When do you need to know by?' (So you can prepare, rather than react.)

'This is happening more quickly than I'd like. Can we establish what we need to cut down to accommodate the new deadline?'

Meet Kate

Kate is quiet, logical and precise. An expert with high standards, Kate loves solving problems and diving deep into detail.

Her colleagues love her thorough eye for detail and attention to quality. She likes to plan ahead and take a systematic approach to her work and will persevere with quiet diligence until the job is done. Objective and logical, she much prefers facts to emotion, analysis to assumption, and research to impulse. If she doesn't know the answer, she'd rather take her time to figure it out than bluff her way through or go with general consensus.

A true professional, working within strict rules and guidelines doesn't phase her. In fact, she prefers knowing where she stands and welcomes the opportunity to bring order and stability with routines and procedures. In social situations she tends to be more private and reserved, seeing little value in casual small talk, but she's not afraid to ask the difficult questions, especially when it comes to analysing risk. In fact, her 101 questions can drive her colleagues mad, especially when they want to move forward quickly, but if you want something done right, you know Kate will leave no stone unturned and no 'i' undotted.

Her focus on high quality and efficiency means she often picks up on details where others glaze over but, as a perfectionist, she reserves her highest standards for herself. She hates being wrong and beats herself up for making mistakes and is likely to spend much more time preparing, analysing and checking her work compared to others. While this generally pushes her to achieve her best, it can also hold her back from taking risks or taking action until she's 100 per cent certain of her own abilities and the situation in hand.

If you're anything like Kate, you'll probably find that:

You enjoy: research, analysis, complex details and in-depth problem solving. To stay motivated, look for opportunities to get involved in longer-term projects that require depth and focus, rather than immediate quick fixes, pursue work that allows you to develop your area of expertise and structure your day and working environment to give you sizeable chunks of time where you can be absorbed in your work, in between smaller tasks and people-facing time.

You're drained by: unpredictability, erratic or emotional people, chaotic environments, conflict, being wrong or unprepared, feeling rushed and having little private time. Proactively agree expectations, outcomes and communication needs with colleagues to reduce the potential for interruptions and reactive working, negotiate time and space to work independently, practise stealth and camouflage, request meeting agendas upfront (explain this is how you can contribute your best ideas) and request time to think when a request puts you on the spot.

You get frustrated by: mistakes, especially when they are a result of slipshod methods, lack of regard for rules or procedure, when people get carried away by enthusiasm, when quality is sacrificed for speed or where your expertise has been overlooked or ignored. Expand your fact finding to what motivates your colleagues (others may value speed, action or people above accuracy). Present your concerns as questions that provide insight to help them achieve their goal. Your eye for detail can be of service rather than a criticism or a road block that halts progress altogether.

Your biggest fears: are likely to be related to being wrong, especially if others criticise your work or spot a mistake, and taking risks when you don't have all the facts. Watch out for your lizard brain when you feel threatened in these areas and be careful not to take mistakes too personally – sometimes things just don't work out and that's not always a bad thing, nor is it your fault.

Things that come naturally to you: in-depth research, complex problem solving, quality assurance, testing, probably anything that involves fine detail and facts. What you're good at and enjoy, others may be actively procrastinating and resisting. Offer to help with the detail and not only will you be doing them a big favour, but you'll also satisfy yourself that it's done properly.

Things to tell your colleagues:

'Would you like me to give that a once over?'

'Shall I take a look into the detail for you?'

'What are the key factors of success here?'

'Can you send me the agenda on Monday so I can be prepared with my best ideas?'

'Let me think this through and come back to you with my questions/comments by Thursday.'

'Let me take this away and work on it. When do you need an update/the finished product by?'

'I'd like to get a full understanding of all the variables so I can crack on with putting the solution together. Rather than go back and forth with meetings and emails, can we book in a morning/afternoon to get it hammered out once and for all?'

Strengths and weaknesses

> 'Everybody is a genius. But if you judge a fish by its ability to climb a tree, it will live its whole life believing that it is stupid.'
>
> ALBERT EINSTEIN

What would come to mind if I asked you about your strengths and weaknesses? You may be tempted to focus on your strengths and ignore or avoid your weaknesses. Or you might find your weaknesses come to mind much more easily, as they are the things you struggle with and stumble at, the things you think you ought to be better at or have resigned yourself to being rubbish at. They are the words you would choose to complete the sentence: 'I'm too...' or 'I'm not very...'. The areas you have spent time, energy, money and attention trying to fix or improve.

Now, I want to ask you, what's the hidden strength in that weakness?

Our strengths and weaknesses are not two separate things. They are two sides of the same coin. Every strength overused becomes a weakness and every weakness hides a strength.

As my friend Marianne Cantwell put it, 'Our weaknesses are just our strengths in the wrong environment.'[1] It's where something we're really good at gets misused, overused or simply used in a place where it isn't appreciated, like Marianne's own love for change and seeking new solutions. It got her into trouble in her old job where she was being paid to follow the status quo, ask no questions and just get the job done, but now her fresh insights and incisive questions are exactly what her Free Range Humans love and value about her and pay her for.

I was bowled over recently by my nine-year-old's teacher at parents evening. There are really only three things I want to know as a parent at parents evening: 1) How's my child doing? 2) Is he in an environment where he can thrive? 3) What can I do to help?

The teacher could have said: 'Yes, he's doing fine, well above what's expected. The only thing he needs to work on is his pace, as he can be a bit slow. This is what you can practise with him at home...' But, instead, he described our son as a thoughtful boy who cares about getting things right, a methodical learner who is hungry to learn and does best when he takes it step by step; a deep thinker you won't hear from for a while, but when he does contribute to a group discussion, he's worth listening to; and a powerful writer whose words are something his teacher looks forward to reading.

Now, that's a teacher who knows my boy. And because of that, his classroom is an environment I know he'll thrive in. If he had focused only on the weakness, we would have known one tiny little fact about who he's not, and missed everything about who he is.

When we focus on our weaknesses, all we notice is who we're not. Where can we really go from there?

Our weaknesses stem from our strengths. They are our strengths overused: when drive becomes stubbornness, when directness becomes rudeness, when compassion becomes people pleasing, when an ability to make stuff happen becomes control freakery, when attention to detail becomes perfectionism, when thoughtful becomes slow, when fast becomes impatient, when improvisation becomes unreliability, when imagination becomes easily distracted, and when possibility becomes indecisiveness.

Our gut instinct is to suppress those weaknesses by changing who we are. But when we focus on our strengths - especially the strength that lies at the heart of each weakness - we can start to channel our strengths in the direction where they will grow healthily instead of spiral out of control. We can harness them in an environment where they will thrive and be valued. We can refine them into something that's brilliant and beautiful rather than destructive.

More than that, our strengths are who we are. When we ignore our strengths, we hide who we really are. We see only a glimpse of who we could be, just a shadow of our strengths, overused or misdirected. When we nurture our strengths, we honour who we are, we learn how to handle ourselves, we grow to become the best of who we can be and we thrive. Boy, do we thrive.

Redefining weakness

What would you consider to be one of your weaknesses? Find the strength that's hidden within and speak it out like it's a good thing.

For example, instead of saying, 'I'm easily distracted by shiny new ideas' how about, 'I have my best ideas at the most unexpected times, so I will make sure I'm always ready to capture them.'

Instead of saying, 'I'm such a perfectionist' try, 'I have high standards and take pride in my work. I may not be the fastest, but I always deliver quality – I just need to remind myself to "deliver" that quality rather than perpetually edit and keep it to myself.'

Harnessing strength

What are your strengths? Where are your strengths most appreciated? What environment do you thrive best in? How often do you get to work in that environment? What changes could you make to your work or the way that you work to operate from a place of strength more often?

What life support or coping strategies do you need to put in place when you are not in that environment? As human beings, we are very adaptable. While spending all your time out of your element is not advised, we can surprise ourselves with how much we can flex outside of our comfort zone when the purpose or situation calls.

What can you do to nurture your strengths? What training could you pursue to develop your strengths? What opportunities would allow you to practise and grow your natural abilities? What support, mentoring or inspiration would feed those strengths

Bear with me

Let's stop thinking we have to be perfect or entirely normal. As human beings, we sometimes defy logic and we all have our own foibles and quirks. That's what makes our contributions and creations more unique. Instead of hiding behind a mask of complete normality, what conversations can you have with those you live and work with?

If you are easily distracted by shiny things, who could you give a heads up to, or permission to call out your magpie behaviour when it's not serving you well? If you find yourself getting bored or bogged down in detail, where would it be appropriate to admit openly that you may not have covered all the angles, who could you hand over the baton to, to cast an eagle eye over the finer details? If you have a tendency to be as subtle as a bull in a china shop, who would it be useful to forewarn that your directness doesn't necessarily mean you have upset, angry, dismissive or combative, but that you just tend to be economical with your words? If you don't think best on your feet, when might it be useful to say, 'Bear with me. I need some time to process this. Let me come back to you.'?

When we are open about our imperfections, quirks and foibles, we can prepare and equip people with insights, tips and strategies on how best to work with us, so that when they notice certain behaviours they have a better understanding of what that might mean (rather than assume what it would mean in their world) and what to do about it. It's not a blank pass to behave however we want, but rather a heads up to avoid offence and miscommunication, to promote better ways of working together and also to give permission for others to call us out when we are not operating in our strengths or when we're overusing our strengths.

What do you need?

Often, we treat other people how we like to be treated, but what about how they'd like to be treated? As an extrovert and a high relater, I thrive on praise – I love getting feedback from people to know that I've helped them. On the other hand, my friend Josie, who is a much more private introvert, would rather avoid feedback, positive or negative. She appreciates that people are trying to make her feel good when they give her feedback, but she still finds that place of being judged incredibly uncomfortable. Ironically, her work often is so good that people can't help but give her praise, but her real joy comes from creating, from the work itself.

Another friend, Rebekah, thrives on fun. She can tackle even the most complex spreadsheets, as long as she's having fun. So her screen and her working environment is full of colour, pretty things, pictures, music and, even, hula hoops because that's what she needs to do her best work.

My husband, on the other hand, is highly sensitive to noise – visual and auditory noise. If he's in a busy environment with lots of sound, stuff and especially people, his senses go into overload and he can't think straight. So what he needs is quiet and space.

What open conversations could you have with the people you work with, to find out what they need to be motivated, to do their best thinking, to know that they are valued or to deal with difficulties, conflict or setbacks? How often do you ask someone, 'What do you need?'?

Basic human needs

Let's go back to basics for a minute. In 1943 Abraham Maslow proposed in his paper 'A Theory of Human Motivation' that there are five hierarchical levels of human needs:

1. **Physiological**: air, food, drink, shelter, warmth, sex, sleep.

2. **Safety**: protection from elements, security, order, law, stability, freedom from fear.

3. **Love and belonging**: friendship, intimacy, affection, love – from work, family, friends, romantic relationships.

4. **Esteem**: achievement, mastery, independence, status, dominance, prestige, self-respect, respect from others.

5. **Self-actualisation**: realising personal potential, self-fulfilment, seeking personal growth and peak experiences.

So, why is it that we think we can sacrifice sleep as long as we have enough self-fulfilment, or that prestige will compensate for a lack of close relationships?

It's true that the higher needs are our true motivators – the more we get, the more it fuels our motivation – whereas the lower levels are what Maslow referred to as 'deficiency needs' – they are strong drivers when they are unmet, but once they are met they no longer fuel us. Once we have enough food or sleep, getting more generally doesn't really excite us! But we do need to meet our basic human needs.

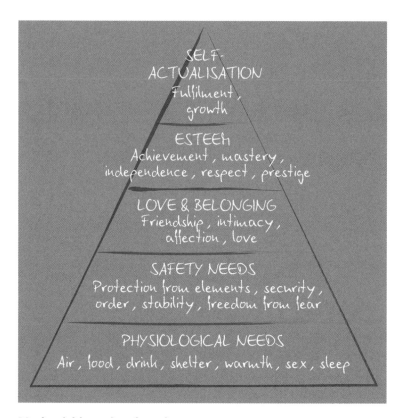

Maslow's hierarchy of needs
Maslow, A. H. (1943), 'A theory of human motivation', *Psychological Review* 50(4), 370–96. This content is in the public domain.

Three basic human needs that often get sidelined in the 'too busy' conversation are:

- sleep
- diet and hydration
- exercise.

Sleep

We all know we need it. But it's often one of the first things to go when we're faced with a crazy schedule, overwhelming workload or an impending deadline. In fact, with comments such as 'I can sleep when I'm dead' and 'the most successful CEOs have only four hours' sleep', it has almost become a competition to see who can get away with the least amount of sleep.

I don't know about you, but I know from both self-induced and baby-induced sleep deprivation that when I don't get enough sleep, I'm more scatterbrained, less focused, easily distracted and lose my train of thought. I do a lot of staring at screens. I forget my words. I'm less engaging as a trainer. I'm less creative and less able to think on my feet. I'm also far more grumpy, more prone to sense-of-humour-failures and far less forgiving – of others and of myself. You know that moment when you see a toddler throwing a tantrum on the floor and the parents turn around to each other and say with that knowing voice 'they're tired'? That happens to us adults, too.

Research increasingly suggests that 'the short-term productivity gains from skipping sleep to work are quickly washed away by the detrimental effects of sleep deprivation on your mood, ability to focus, and access to higher-level brain functions for days to come. The negative effects of sleep deprivation are so great that people who are drunk outperform those lacking sleep.'[2]

Lack of sleep affects our high-level brain function: our ability to think logically, process information, pay attention and think creatively – all the things we need to do our work well. It affects our mood, resilience and relationships – making us more easily irritated or upset, less objective, more likely to take things personally, more prone to misunderstanding and more reactive to stress. It affects our health: from colds that take weeks to shake, headaches, coughs, infections, loss of voice (a highly inconvenient occupational hazard for teachers and trainers), existing conditions that get triggered (my husband's bad back gets aggravated by lack of sleep) to more serious health conditions – cancer, heart disease, Type 2 diabetes, infections and obesity have all been linked to reduced sleep.[3]

It also affects our memory and routines: forgetting to put the milk in the porridge, losing keys in the fridge, forgetting to lock the door, missing the turning that you take every single day to work – things we take for granted and usually do without thinking, we forget to do when we're tired. And we become more prone to making mistakes. As my husband found when he completely killed a database he was trying to fix after pulling an all-nighter: we can do more damage than good when we're tired. Bill Clinton, who has made some pretty famous mistakes, said on CNN in 2008:

> 'Most of the mistakes I made, I made when I was too tired, because I tried too hard and worked too hard. You make better decisions when you're not too tired.'[4]

Diet and hydration

Convenience food, skipping meals, surviving on a diet of chocolate and coffee – we've all done it when we're pressed for time, but this too can be a quick fix that ends up costing us more.

Going hungry doesn't help. If you put 'hunger' as one of your culprits for distraction in Chapter 2, you'll be pleased to know that you have scientific backing. Your brain needs fuel to function and that fuel is glucose, twenty-five grams of glucose in fact – 'about the amount found in a banana', according to brain researcher Leigh Gibson.[5]

How you get that glucose doesn't affect brain function immediately, but quick-release sugars will cause spikes and slumps in glucose levels that mess with our ability to concentrate – which explains why it's so hard to stay awake in meetings that occur straight after a carb-heavy lunch, and why eating sugary foods makes you crave more. Whereas slow-release foods, such as oats, or combining sugar with protein, will give a more steady level of focus and attention. Personally, I've found that being on a sugar high might not have me bouncing on furniture like my children do, but it certainly makes me more jumpy and easily distracted.

'Adequate nutrition can raise your productivity levels by 20 per cent on average', according to the World Health Organisation, which recommends dark chocolate, nuts and seeds as great foods to snack on for productivity.

Dehydration also affects our productivity. The human brain is made up of 75 per cent water, and even mild dehydration can affect our mental performance as well as our mood and physical energy. It's often said that once you're thirsty, it's already too late. If you're feeling sluggish or foggy, the chances are you may well be dehydrated.

Exercise

Exercising releases endorphins, makes us happier and keeps our bodies active and healthy – and it also gets our brains working better. Brain activity increases after a 20-minute walk, compared to sitting still, and a study by the University of Bristol found that, 'On exercise days, people's mood significantly improved after exercising. Mood stayed about the same on days they didn't, with the exception of people's sense of calm which deteriorated.'

Many clients and workshop delegates I've worked with have reported that doing some exercise before work or during the working day has helped them to be more charged, focused and creative in their work. Taking a walk or even just standing up can change our brain activity and get us thinking differently. The same goes for walking meetings and stand-up meetings. Changing our physiology changes our thinking. Our brains have evolved to solve problems on the move:

> 'Exercise physically remodels our brains for peak performance... and is essential for helping the brain and body recover from stress, learning and cognitive renewal'
>
> PROFESSOR JOHN RATEY[6]

Safety, love and belonging

It's also worth remembering that safety, love and belonging needs are also essential needs in the pyramid. Our sense of security and certainty and the health and quality of our relationships at work also affect our productivity. Working in a hostile or toxic environment can be a real productivity killer – however personally motivated or brilliantly organised you are. Operating in a season of high-level unpredictability and insecurity will take its toll in energy and attention. Major life changes, from getting married, having children and moving house to divorce, bereavement and family issues, all have an impact on how we show up at work.

Pretending these things don't affect us can consume valuable attention and energy that's already in short supply. Giving ourselves and our colleagues permission to show up as human is far more effective for our well-being and our productivity, and when we have the opportunity to support each other as fellow human beings, we create strong working relationships and genuine friendships that transform both the quality of our work and the quality of our life at work.

One-point improvements

We all know this to a degree, but how do we get back on track? It's one thing to know that looking after our physical needs will improve our productivity, but how do we change our habits when life is busy and short-cutting on our basic needs has become an accepted way of life? Here are some ways to get started with small steps:

- Create a relaxing bedtime routine.

- Aim for one early night a week.

- Try a screen-free evening.

- Bulk-cook meals and freeze in portions.

- Stock fruit, nuts and dark chocolate as snacks.

- Have a glass of water next to your bed; drink it before you get up in the morning.

- Keep a drink of water on your desk (a friend of mine even used her 'coffee to go' cup for this).

- Take phone calls standing up.

- Get a stand-up desk or an adjustable one.

- Have walking or stand-up meetings.

- Take a walk at lunch-times.

- Do desk stretches.

- Keep a stock of healthy breakfast supplies at work.

- Encourage healthy eating at work with an office weekly shop where healthy snacks come out of the office budget and unhealthy snacks are paid for by the individuals themselves.

- Have a shower at the office for those who want to cycle to work or go for a lunch-time run.

- ....

- ....

What do you need to give yourself?

This is a question I often ask my clients, and one that has two parts:

1. What do you need?

2. What do you give yourself?

Do you always give yourself what you need? How often do you give yourself a hard time, when what you really need is a break – or distraction when what you really need is focus? Do you give yourself more to worry about when what you need is clarity? Do you give yourself criticism when what you really need is encouragement?

What do you need to give yourself to be at your best?

Because when you're at your best, you do your best work and you give your best to whoever you're with – at work, at home and everywhere else in life.

Over to you

Questions to ask yourself

My motivation:

What do I enjoy?

....

What motivates me?

....

What gets the best out of me?

....

Where I'm likely to procrastinate:

What drains me?

....

What frustrates me?

....

What do I fear?

....

My ideal environment:

How do I work best?

....

What changes can I make to my current environment?

....

....

My strengths:

What are my strengths?

....

What comes naturally to me?

....

Where is that most appreciated?

....

My weaknesses:

What are my vulnerabilities and blindspots?

....

What's the hidden strength?

....

How I communicate:

What do others need to know about me?

....

My needs:

What do I need in order to be at my best?

....

What do I need to give myself?

....

What do I need to ask for?

....

One-point improvements to meet my basic human needs are:

....

Questions to discuss with your team

What are our individual and collective strengths?

....

....

How do we complement each other?

....

....

How do we potentially get in each other's way?

....

....

Where are our potential blind spots?

....

....

Where can we cover each other?

....

....

Are there any gaps?

....

....

What do we need to request from each other? ('Please give me...')

....

....

What do we need to ask for grace on? ('Bear with me when...')

....

....

Chapter 8

Work–life rhythm

D oes a 9–5 job still exist? Is there life outside of work? Are you working from home or living at work? With technology, mobility and increasingly global work teams, the boundaries around work are blurring and the quest for work–life balance has become both more insistent and elusive.

The truth is, there is life at work and life outside of work and our productivity depends on us nurturing both. How do you develop a routine that's both consistent and flexible? How do you work with relentless focus and switch off at the end of the day? How do you stay motivated and on fire without burning out? How do you keep going and how do you stop? This chapter will challenge the traditional notion of work–life balance and give you tools to answer all these questions and more.

Beyond the 9–5

Does the 9–5 job still exist? For most people I know – friends, family, clients, colleagues – it's a myth. From teachers who work up to nearly 60 hours a week[1] to senior directors who regularly spend 30–40 hours just in meetings, then try and catch up on emails and the 'real work' at home. Even for those whose hours are less extreme, many people admit to staying a little later, arriving a little earlier, and taking work home to 'catch up'.

Longer hours don't work

The law of diminishing returns states that not every extra hour put in will generate the same output. Henry Ford's experiments on productivity found that 40 hours per week was the optimum number of hours for his production-line employees. When they worked past those 40 hours, their productivity would diminish.

For work that requires intense focus, this number is even less. Most creators and writers find that they have only a couple of hours of proactive attention when they're at their best, coming up with their best ideas, doing their best work. After that, they can work on other stuff – but their attention levels are nowhere near the same.

We all have our optimum level of working. Beyond that, each extra hour we put in will cost more and give us less in return.

Flexibility

With the increase of flexible working and 24/7 technology, the lines that used to define work have become blurred. This gives us a challenge and an opportunity.

The opportunity is that it gives us flexibility. With increasing flexibility we get to define our own hours. We can choose to get to the office earlier to avoid the rush-hour traffic or later to fit in the school run. We can take ourselves for a run at lunch-time because it clears our mind and forms part of our marathon training. We can fit in that meeting for the social enterprise we're setting up while we're in London for work. We can negotiate flexible working from home to fit around care commitments, or work on the beach whilst travelling. We can pursue part-time study or set up our own business without quitting the job that pays the bills.

The challenge is also that it gives us flexibility. It's up to us to define our hours, when everything is possible and there are no set rules to fall back on. We need to choose our hours rather than end up working all hours. It's easy to do that one extra hour, send that one last email, say yes to that one extra commitment, check that one last time when it is already way past your bedtime. It's hard to say, 'I'm not at work right now' when your work follows you wherever you go. And when others are practising flexibility, we can find ourselves adopting their hours as well as our own – if my boss is emailing me at 7 am on Saturday morning, does that mean I should be replying then, too?

Working from home or living at work?

I love working from home. I know, it's not for everyone. Some people find it hard to switch off from home life to focus on work. They get distracted by the washing up, the door handle that needs fixing and other jobs around the house.

Me, I happily close the door to the laundry, shove the washing up to one side, clear a space at my kitchen table and start working away in my own little bubble. Give me work over housework any day. Give me pretty much anything over housework, though, come to think of it.

I love the flexibility and the freedom. To work around my children, do the school runs, make it to sports days and school plays, and still get my work done and do my job well. It gives me the chance to make the best of both worlds, do work and life on my own terms. And I definitely don't miss the commute.

That's the plan, right?

So what happens when we find ourselves sending emails at the dinner table, taking urgent phone calls while bathing the kids, repeating 'just a minute' on loop while we try and get that one thing done, or when we stop making eye contact with our partner and the laptop has become a permanent extension to our legs?

Is this really the work-from-home dream? Or are we just living at work? What's the difference, really, between this and pulling a late-nighter at the office?

Measure impact, not hours

It's hard to count the hours. If I asked you how many hours you worked last week, you might work out the times you arrived and left the office or your desk, the times when you have kids in childcare or the part of your diary marked as work time, but what about the times when you were checking your emails, taking calls, travelling, booking train tickets or mentally preparing for your next meeting? And did you remember to take off the dentist appointment, the time when you were on hold to the mobile phone company while keeping half an eye on your emails, or had coffee with a networking contact who also happens to be a good friend (which category does that fall under?). And, if you did do all that, where would the 'counting time' time be allocated to?

Perhaps this is the perfect opportunity to move away from face time (putting in the hours just to show your face at work) to productive work (focusing on what matters, getting it done in as much or as little time as you need).

At Think Productive our Productivity Ninjas are, essentially, freelancers and contractors – we work when we want, where we want and how we want, and we get paid by results – by the business we bring in and training we deliver. But even companies with salaried employees recognise that focusing on results and trusting their employees to work out how they achieve them not only improves productivity, but morale, creativity and market results too.

Both Netflix and Virgin have ditched the idea of tracking working hours – both on a day-to-day basis and even when it comes to vacation. 'We should focus on what people get done, not how many hours or days worked. Just as we don't have a 9–5 day policy, we don't need a vacation policy', says Netflix in their 'Reference Guide on our Freedom & Responsibility Culture'.[2]

As Richard Branson explains,

> **'It is left to the employee alone to decide if and when he or she feels like taking a few hours, a day, a week or a month off, the assumption being that they are only going to do it when they feel 100-per-cent comfortable that they and their team are up to date on every project and that their absence will not in any way damage the business – or, for that matter, their careers!'[3]**

If you are reading this thinking, 'Well, it would be ok if I worked for Netflix or Virgin!', it's worth noting that, even at Virgin, this doesn't extend to the entire Virgin empire. Reading through the comments on that particular post, there are examples of cabin crew in Virgin Australia who don't have the same experience, but there's also an example of a hospital in Canada that has implemented an unlimited vacation policy.

Whichever way you look at it, it's a start. And my question to you is, where could you start?

Where could you start to influence and steer your productivity conversations from measuring time to measuring impact?

Work and life

Work and life are not two separate entities. There's life at work and life outside of work. There's work at work and work outside of work. There's our life's work. There's making life work. There's work that brings you to life.

Work and life are not mutually exclusive, so why do we insist on balancing them like equal opposites on a scale?

Beyond work–life balance

Most people I work with say they want a better work–life balance. They want to be productive at work so that they can go home on time, 'switch off' and have a life outside of work.

But I have a problem with the term 'work–life balance'. I have a problem with it because, in reality, it has become this holy grail that no one seems to get.

It's supposed to get us working less and enjoying life more but, in reality, it has us striving for perfection and counting the hours we spend at work, the hours we spend with our family, at the gym, even in bed, trying to get the elusive 'right' combination.

It's created a superhero syndrome, where it's no longer good enough to be good at just one thing. We have to be great at everything: flying high at work, going the extra mile and exceeding expectations, raising great kids, giving them brilliant childhood experiences, helping them with homework and extra reading, feeding them healthy, nutritious organic homemade food, having the best marriage, going on luxurious holidays, volunteering for the school PTA, board of governors or some other community involvement and all the while having an immaculate home. We have to be all things to all people and it's exhausting just thinking about it!

It has also become a source of guilt. We're constantly counting the hours that go by and worrying that we're not spending enough time elsewhere (more about that in Chapter 9).

The problem with work–life balance is we have turned something that was intended to give us a break into something we beat ourselves up with. Perhaps it's time to let go of work–life balance. It was a man-made invention after all.

Here are some alternative propositions instead.

Work–life rhythm

Having a work-life rhythm means there are highs and lows and ebbs and flows to your life, instead of trying to make everything uniform and balanced. There are times when we need to run fast and times when we need to slow down and be still.

So, instead of trying to slow down the fast times and speed up the slow, let's run with life when it speeds up. Let's treat rest and renewal as essential to our productivity. Let's embrace the wild rides, soak up the quiet lulls and enjoy everything in between.

We are, after all, human beings and not robots. We physically (and mentally) cannot sustain the same level of performance through every hour of the day. Studies into ultradian rhythm show our natural biology works best in cycles of 90–120 minutes, followed by times of rest and renewal.

Work–life integrity

Are you the same person at work and outside of work? Yes, you may adapt your behaviour to suit the situation but, deep down, are you being the same person, with the same values, identity and purpose?

Work–life integrity is not so much to do with the hours we spend, but who we are being at work. When we are true to ourselves at work, there's a sense of peace that comes with it.

When there's a conflict with our core values, no matter how much we achieve, our work will lack meaning and satisfaction and our life will feel out of balance.

The same applies to life outside of work. For those of us fortunate to find ourselves doing work that we love, sometimes the challenge is to be the same fired-up, passionate person at home, with grumpy teenagers and tired toddlers, when we might be equally tired and grumpy ourselves.

As I heard one CEO admit recently, 'People at work thank us more, they appreciate our contributions, they think we're brilliant. I can't always say the same for my family!'

I realised a while ago that to truly live up to my 'Chief Encourager' title in my business, I need to make sure I'm encouraging my children just as much as I encourage my clients. On a practical level, this means having reserves of energy and patience beyond working hours, making sure I set healthy boundaries and get enough sleep, so that my children don't just get the leftovers at the end of the day.

Work–life integrity is about being equally mindful of who we are being both at work and outside of work, so that the way we live and work honours the values that matter most to us.

Work–life quality

We all have crazy seasons, when one part of our life takes over the others, but just because we don't have as much time for the other parts of our life, it doesn't mean we can't enjoy them as much.

One week I spent five hours travelling on a Sunday in order to deliver a workshop the following Monday, which meant that I had only a short weekend with my family. Determined to make the most of it, we enjoyed a lazy morning together as a family, taking our time over an indulgent pancake brunch before my train journey. What we lacked in quantity, we more than made up for in quality.

The quality of our life at work matters, too. Hours are not the only way to measure how consuming our work can be. Conflict, difficult relationships, lack of appreciation, lack of connection or community, uncertainty, stress and being constantly overwhelmed can all contribute to a low quality of life at work that takes far more out of us than time spent in a positive, productive environment.

Instead of obsessing over hours, let's make sure the quality of life at work and life outside of work is good. Because when our life at work is good, we are naturally more productive and happier at home. When our life at home is good, the quality of our work improves. Our well-being and productivity are inextricably linked, both in and outside of work.

Daily rhythms

As human beings our energy levels vary throughout the day. We are not designed to be turned on and off, with a constant output like a machine. We have peaks and troughs, times when we're fully switched on and raring to go, and times when we're more mellow, more easily distracted or even completely zonked – and that's completely normal and natural. Instead of trying to change that, let's try and work with it.

Know your patterns

Are you an early bird or a night owl? My daughter is an early bird. She wakes up with a zing and practically bounces out of bed with a smile on her face and a spring in her step, coming into our room saying, 'What are we doing today?'. My son, on the other hand, takes a lot longer to wake up. He goes slow in the mornings and comes alive in the evenings. Typically, when it's time to go to bed, he will be full of energy, chatting about everything under the sun.

When are you at your best? When's your prime time? What do you do with that time?

If you are a morning person, do you reserve the mornings to do your best work - the things that require your best attention? Or does your morning get frittered away with emails, phone calls and other people's agendas?

My best friend is not a morning person at all. It takes her most of the morning to fully wake up. She has found that using her morning to do the things that don't require her best energy - point-and-click stuff, form filling, filing, quick wins and bitty jobs - clears the clutter so that when she's fully on form in the afternoon, she can focus her best energy on the things that really matter.

In *How to be a Productivity Ninja*, Graham Allcott suggests thinking about your attention levels in three categories:

1. **Proactive** attention (when you're on full form).

2. **Active** attention (awake, reasonably alert).

3. **Inactive** attention (brain dead, zombie mode, physically here but no one's home).

Your attention levels will vary during the day - being aware of them means you can decide what's best to tackle in each mode. As Graham puts it, 'You'll start to realise that it's a criminal waste to be changing the printer cartridge during a period of proactive attention. It's like using a sledgehammer to crack a nut, although in that moment it probably feels no different to when you change the printer cartridge at any other time.'

Know your landscape

Your energy and attention levels don't just depend on the time of day. They also vary according to what else is going on around that time. Have you had a day full of meetings or a heavy week of travelling? Are you battling the flu or do you have a child who is battling sleep? That's likely to affect your energy and attention levels.

What else have you got in your diary or on your to-do list? Are they tasks and activities that energise you or drain you? If my husband has a people-intensive week, the chances are he'll be pretty exhausted. If I've spent a morning staring at spreadsheets, I will have very little attention left for screen-work, whereas I'd positively welcome a coaching conversation or a networking meeting.

DO THE CANDLE TEST

I first came across this exercise when I did my NLP training with Tony Burgess and Julie French, and it's one I often use with clients.[4]

Draw a candle.

Next to the flame, make a list of tasks, activities and environments that energise you. What makes you come alive? What do you enjoy doing so much that it gives you energy? Write those things down next to the flame.

Next to the wax, make a note of tasks and activities that drain you. What takes energy out of you? What leaves you drained? They could be things you are perfectly competent and perhaps even very good at doing but, ultimately, if you do too much of it, you end up running on empty.

Now use this to gauge your day or week ahead. How much of your time and energy are you spending 'in the flame'? How much are you spending 'in the wax'? How does this affect your energy levels?

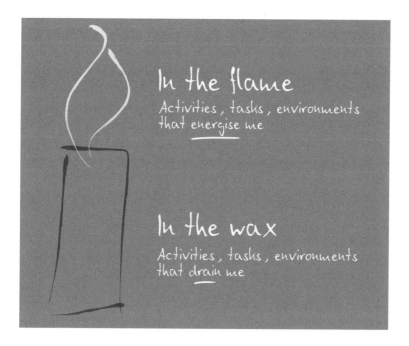

In the flame
Activities, tasks, environments that energise me

In the wax
Activities, tasks, environments that drain me

To improve your energy and create a more sustainable rhythm, consider the following questions:

- How could you spend more time 'in the flame' and less time 'in the wax'?
- Is the wax supporting your flame or drowning it?
- What flame activity could you introduce to brighten up a 'waxy' day?
- How could you mix and match your 'flame' and 'wax' activities to regulate your energy levels during the day?
- What could you move from the 'wax' into the 'flame' by changing the way you work? (For example, if business planning drains you but being outdoors gives you energy, could you take your planning session outdoors and combine it with a walk?)

Starting the day well

How do you start the day? Do you stumble out of bed and go through the motions like a zombie? Do you race around tending to a million-and-one things clambering for your attention from the moment your alarm goes off? Do you slide the alarm off on your phone and go straight into your emails?

How do you wake up?

Some people swear by their early-morning workouts – it gets their blood pumping and their brains and bodies working first thing in the morning. I have to admit, the days when I do manage to go for a 7 am run, I feel great! Other people prefer a much gentler start – perhaps with a slow stretch or some peaceful meditation. A quiet cup of tea with their brains to themselves – perhaps in one of those cups that say 'shh... don't talk to me yet'.

One of my friends found that sitting up in bed, doing some gentle stretches and drinking a glass of water before getting up helped her to wake up properly before going into 'do' mode. Another friend found that getting out of bed as soon as the alarm went off, instead of staying in bed for 'just a few minutes more', helped to snap her out of her morning lethargy. My colleague Katy recently discovered that power posing[5] in bed for 5–10 minutes before she got up in the morning made her feel a lot happier, more energised and less groggy.

Getting into work mode

Our brains are wired up to notice patterns and signals. What signals trigger your brain to switch between home mode and work mode? If you travel to an office, the commute might be when that transition happens. If you work from home, however, you might need to create or recreate that signal.

A financial advisor I know was relishing the prospect of ditching his suit when he started working from home, to find that it was only when he put his tie on that he felt at work. Another friend created his own commute by walking round the block each morning and evening to start and finish his work day. My husband even found that when he started working from home, drinking from a designated work cup helped to put him in work mode!

Of course, there's nothing wrong with working in your pyjamas, as long as you find your own way of getting into work mode. Think about the little things you could do to give yourself those signals that it's time to get to work, from simple things like having breakfast or having a shave to putting on a piece of music, listening to your regular morning radio show or meditating for 10 minutes.

Check in with yourself first

It's tempting to check your emails first thing in the morning. Especially if you have your smartphone doubling up as an alarm, on charge next to your bed. But when you check in with the rest of the world before checking in with yourself, it's very easy to let someone else's agenda dictate your day. One piece of bad news can set the mood and tone of your day. One unforeseen problem or opportunity can take you on a tangent before you have had a chance to decide what's really important from your perspective.

The world is full of messages. It's amazing how easy it is to be buffeted from one thing to another when you're not clear on your own agenda, and you spend the day reacting to whoever or whatever is shouting the loudest. One thing I often encourage clients to do is to have half an hour in the morning to check in with themselves first, before they check in with the rest of the world.

For example:

- Writing your 'hit list' for the day – your top one to three 'must do's' – on a Post-it Note before turning on your email.

- Setting your email to open up to Calendar or Task View as a default, rather than the Inbox.

- If you are a Google Chrome user, check out the Momentum extension, where you can set your focus for the day and be inspired and reminded of it every time you open a new browser tab.

Choose your focus

The other day, I didn't want to get up. It was grey and wet outside and I was warm and sleepy in my bed. I was tired when I got up, when I got the kids ready, when I questioned why yet again we were trying to find stuff when it was time to go, when I marched my daughter straight into a puddle outside her classroom because I didn't notice it because I was tired.

I realised I needed to choose something, otherwise tiredness would choose me. I chose to wake up. I chose to go for a run in the pouring rain, which was strangely refreshing once I abandoned the notion of staying dry! I made my neighbour smile and the road-workers too, which made me smile (always happy to be of service.) It worked: I woke up. I was still tired, but I was awake and alive – and that made a big difference to me and my day.

What about you? If you don't fancy a run in the rain, never in a million years, that's all right. It's your choice, and that's the point.

If you've got a clear day in front of you, what are you choosing to fill it with? If you have a busy day ahead, packed full of commitments, how are you choosing to approach it? With panic or enthusiasm, dread or determination? That difficult conversation you need to have: what will you choose? Patience? Compassion? Assertiveness? Bullishness?

The stressful environment at work, where everyone is feeling the pressure and sniping at each other – will you choose to join in or buck the trend and be the one who smiles contagiously? That thing that takes you outside your comfort zone – will you choose avoidance, reluctance or will you choose to throw yourself in fully? The situation beyond your control, the one that's painful, difficult and unavoidable – will you choose to live in frustration and disappointment or in courage, hope, faith, kindness, humour or the company of good friends around you?

Whatever's going on, you always have a choice. Sometimes it's a big choice, sometimes it's a little one. Sometimes it will transform the world around you. Other times it will just transform you.

What are you choosing for today?

Maintaining momentum (or what to do when the work never ends)

'Every day I start with a bulging to-do list, full of energy and optimism to charge ahead. Come on, bring it on, let's do this thing. By lunch-time my energy starts waning and the end is nowhere near in sight. By the end of the day, I'm knackered, disappointed, bewildered (where did the time go?) and proceed to shuffle what's left to an already full list for tomorrow.'

When the work never ends, it can be hard to find momentum and motivation and it's easy for inertia and procrastination to set in. After all, if there's just more work ahead, what's the incentive for getting on with it and getting it done? On the other hand, we can find ourselves constantly working and never stopping and, somewhere along the line, we lose our interest, our passion and our joy. The work we love becomes drudgery and we burn out.

When the work never ends, it's up to us to create our own finish lines, to define for ourselves what 'job done' looks like.

Without a finish line, it's easy to lose momentum and for the project to creep. The product is never quite ready to be launched, the website still needs tweaking, the Search Engine Optimisation (SEO) campaign becomes so long and arduous, you find yourself reluctantly trudging along rather than powering through.

Without a finish line, it's easy to get distracted by shiny things, 'I'll just take a look at this first' or quick wins, 'I'll just deal with this first... oh, and that one...' and get stalled by the enormity of it all, 'Woah! That's a long way to go. I'm going to have to wait until I have more time. Better make that cup of tea...'

When there's a finish line in sight, you've got something to aim for. It gives you direction, definition and a reason to muster up the strength and to sprint ahead.

Freya was someone who had a tendency to go all guns blazing at the beginning of a project, full of enthusiasm and adrenaline, so much so that, in those early days, it wouldn't be unusual for her to get more done than she set out to do. She'd power through her to-do list, find she still had time left in the day and add a few more jobs in. But after a while she'd burn out. She would run out of energy and start becoming aware of everything else in life she had put on hold, then wonder how on earth she could ever fit it all in.

When she came on my '40 Days of Baby Steps' programme, she set herself a goal to get a whole list of things done before the summer holidays, but instead of going as fast as she could for as long as she could, she decided to pace herself and honour a daily finish line when she would be 'done for the day'. Whenever she got to the end of her to-do list, she gave herself permission to stop. Instead of doing just one more thing, she took a break, clocked off early, celebrated 'done' and enjoyed the time for herself.

The result? She found herself with far more energy throughout the 40 days. Instead of running as fast as she could for the first couple of days and then running out of steam, she was able to keep pace and keep going. Yes, there were peaks and troughs during that time – some weeks were more productive than others – but, ultimately, she procrastinated less, got more done, took more breaks and enjoyed greater satisfaction. She got everything done that she wanted to get done before the summer holidays and proved to herself that she could do it without killing herself.

The bad news is the work never ends. But the good news is we get to create our own finish lines. We get to define what 'job done' looks like. When we honour those finish lines, when we enjoy life beyond the finish line, each race is satisfying and we find we have more than enough to keep going.

Where's your finish line each day? When are you done for the day?

Switching off, fuelling up

> 'Almost everything will work again if you unplug it for a few minutes, including you.'
>
> ANNE LAMOTT

Sometimes our brains need actively distracting from work. It can be easy to physically leave the office, close down our laptops and still be at work in our heads. We often associate productivity with work: a productive day usually is a day when we've set goals, got things done, worked hard and achieved what we set out to do. But how do you spend your down time?

Is it more of an afterthought – something you'll figure out once you get there, if you get there? Is it something you put off, telling yourself, 'I'll take time off when I've got everything done'? Do you cram it full of chores and odd jobs. 'Day off: laundry, fix door, get hair cut, buy Christmas presents, pay electricity bill, sort out filing pile, wash car...'

Often, we see our down time as unproductive and, to an extent, unimportant. We downplay it, delay it, avoid it and, when we do find ourselves with it, we don't know what to do with it. We've forgotten how to deal with down time, let alone how to value it, so much so that we're more likely to feel guilty, struggle to justify, or even apologise for having some down time – which is completely and utterly ridiculous.

To recharge is to restore your capacity. Without charge there is no productivity. Recharging is productive. Recharging is not a luxury. It's fuel for our productivity.

The wobbly line

Nobody understands this more than athletes. When an athlete finishes a match, a game or a race, the last thing they will do is go straight back in the gym, onto another match or into more training. It would be completely unthinkable. Athletes understand something that often the rest of us overlook: that recovery is a crucial part of our job. What we do when we're not performing directly impacts how well we perform.

Our tendency to work under pressure without any breaks is completely counterproductive.

Psychologist and workplace resilience specialist Rob Archer asks, 'How wobbly is your line?[6] As human beings we are designed to have periods of high performance followed by periods of recovery, activity followed by rest, and breaks in between the work. Our natural rhythm follows a "wobbly line" that goes up and down. That's how we sustain peak performance and health.'

How wobbly is your line? Does it go up and down? Or does it just flat line (which is never a good sign with anything living!)?

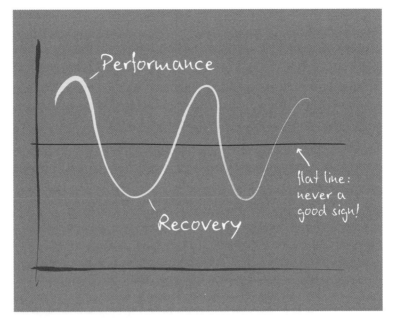

How wobbly is your line?

To work and live well we need to have a rhythm of recovery – daily, weekly, monthly, seasonally – even yearly; time away from the work to recharge so we come back fully fuelled rather than running on empty.

Standby

How do you spend your down time? Do you actually recharge – or do you just go on standby, waiting to get back to work again? Get home, down tools, veg out, sit in front of the telly, surf the net, play some inane game – anything that doesn't require brainpower, but keeps your brain occupied enough that it doesn't completely shut down or start firing up again.

It's an easy option and doesn't require much thought or setting up. You can do it pretty much anywhere, especially if you have Candy Crush on your phone (ahem). And it does conserve energy to a degree, but only gives minimal recharge, if any at all.

There are certain things I know I default to that put me on standby rather than actually recharge me. I know because I get pulled towards them for that instant light relief, but a couple of hours later I feel just as drained as I did before – except it's now later and I'm a couple of hours closer to when I need to be back on form.

Solitude vs. company

My husband is a strong introvert. This means he recharges when he's alone. He loves spending time with family and friends and enjoys a good conversation (especially of the techie kind), but when he's had a full on week, especially a week full of people, he needs his time alone.

We call it his cave time, which might be in the garage, out on his motorbike, going for a walk or taking a trip somewhere. It doesn't matter where he goes, as long as he's alone. Without it, he gets grumpy, cranky and can't think straight. Once he's had it, he's recharged, ready and raring to go again. A conversation we have on a regular basis, when we're comparing diaries to work out the logistics of school runs and childcare, is: 'When's your next cave time?' Quite a few introvert leaders I know schedule-in solitude – a weekend every 6 weeks or a 24-hour period once a month, for example, that they block out in the diary in advance and commit to as an essential part of their rhythm.

I'm an extrovert. Generally speaking, I find the company of people energising. I can come away from an evening of lively conversation with friends with more energy than before, especially if I've been desk-bound all day with little human interaction. I'm very blessed that most of my work is with people – speaking, training, coaching – but when I have weeks that are more heavily loaded with proposals, spreadsheets and fiddling with my website, I deliberately schedule in coffee, lunch or a run with a friend to recharge.

Having said that, even though being with people energises me, I still need time to myself. I never really realised this until I had children and found myself in a situation where I was never alone and started craving even just five minutes to myself. So nowadays, when I look at my diary and see back-to-back workshops booked in, I make sure I have a clear day of quiet recovery to catch up with myself (extrovert disclosure: this probably would involve reading a book in a café surrounded by people doing their own thing, rather than being in a cave completely by myself!).

Retreat

What a funny word. In a battle, when someone shouts, 'Retreat!', you get the sense that things are not going so well. It is a last resort, a failure, a sign of weakness. When I think of a spa retreat, though, or a writer's retreat, I think indulgence. It's something I relish, enjoy and welcome. It's an opportunity to rest from the day to day and time to indulge and nurture a part of me – whether that's my dry skin, my inner peace or my writing geek.

What would be a retreat for you? Something that indulges you and feeds your soul? A writing retreat certainly wouldn't be one for my husband, but being surrounded by an engine in bits, tools and absolutely no deadline probably would be more his thing. Some weekends I like to retreat to my kitchen and cook an unhurried meal, while for some of my friends this would be akin to torture. In fact, some of my friends would consider running through mud and swimming in a freezing cold lake the perfect retreat!

Recreation

Recharging is not always about rest (although it doesn't happen without some kind of rest). Sometimes it's about doing something active. For me, a good run can do wonders for my energy. Spending time with friends, laughing, being outdoors, singing, reading, cooking, dancing, jumping on the trampoline, going down a zip wire with my children – these are all things that require me to do something – and they recharge me all the same.

I'm on a rota to sing backing vocals in my church worship band. To me it's not an obligation or another thing to do – it's an honour to serve, yes, and a commitment I take seriously, but it's also one of the ways I recharge. What do you enjoy doing so much that it leaves you feeling more alive and recharged than before? What activities, company and environments actively energise you?

Fuel

What fires you up? What charges your creativity and motivation? What fuels you? Twenty minutes watching a TED talk, a geek-out conversation over lunch or taking a day to attend a conference and network with inspiring people reminds me why I'm doing what I'm doing and does wonders for my motivation and productivity. What's fuel for you? Where do you go for it? How often do you tap into it?

Twenty tiny moments of joy

Psychologist Rob Archer notes:

> **'Everybody gets tired, but exhaustion is different. Classically our reaction to being exhausted is to cut back on the things that give us meaning, purpose and joy. We disengage to conserve our energy, but when we do that, we squeeze out the joy in life and all that remains is the treadmill – and when you combine exhaustion with lack of joy, that's fertile ground for burnout and ill health.'**

One exercise I learned early on in my coaching career was to compile a list of 20 tiny things that bring you joy. Not big things like 'when I'm on top of Mount Kilimanjaro' or 'when I got married', but tiny things such as smelling freshly cut flowers or the way your dog screws up his face when you scratch his head. Tiny things you can do, have or experience in the day to day that bring you joy.

Start your list now – what would your 20 tiny things be?

1. ....
2. ....
3. ....
4. ....
5. ....
6. ....
7. ....
8. ....
9. ....
10. ....
11. ....
12. ....
13. ....
14. ....
15. ....
16. ....
17. ....
18. ....
19. ....
20. ....

The art of slowing down

I'm not one for doing things slowly. My natural, impatient tendency is to go for fast, plenty, varied, active and energised. I'd much rather speed up than slow down. This has served me well over the years. I had my mid-life crisis in my mid-twenties and now wholeheartedly love my work, instead of spending the next 20 years stuck in a job I was trying my best to love.

I've taken giant leaps of faith outside my comfort zone by saying yes more quickly than my lizard brain could say fear. And my whole foray into the world of productivity started because I didn't want to wait until my children were grown up before I pursued my business. Essentially, impatience is what got me good at getting things done.

But lately I've started to wonder if I'm missing a trick and I'm starting to play with the art of slowing down. In the world of productivity, we often talk about getting things done faster, smarter, easier. But what about slower? Here are six areas where slowing down could, in fact, improve our productivity.

Decisions

My fastest decisions are not always my best decisions. Granted, there are times when I need to think on my feet and plenty of times when I just need to pick something, rather than get bogged down in analysis paralysis (just ask my husband when we eat out!). But there have also been times when I've made a quick 'that will do' decision that has ended up costing more to fix or change, once I'd had time to think through what I really wanted.

Planning

Tim Ferris, author of *The 4 Hour Work Week*, said:

> **'Slow down and remember this: most things make no difference. Being busy is a form of mental laziness – lazy thinking and indiscriminate action.'**

We know this. We know that activity does not equal productivity and busyness does not equal business. But there's still something incredibly seductive about being busy because being busy feels productive. And, conversely, thinking time does not. As a workshop delegate put it, 'I always feel like I'm wasting time when I stop and think. I feel like I should just get on with it.'

It's only when we slow down and give ourselves time to think that we notice the difference between getting things done and getting the right things done (and doing them well), and ask ourselves the really incisive questions such as 'what am I actually doing here?'. It's only then that thinking time starts to feel productive.

Communication

They say never send an email when you are angry or in a rush. It is so much easier to make a mistake, send the wrong thing to the wrong person or say something you'll regret. We've all had a laugh at humorous typing errors and hilarious autocorrect conversations. We've probably had our fair share of horror stories, too – where a rushed or reactive email has resulted in confusion, embarrassment, offence or outright war.

Slowing down gives our logical brains a chance to catch up with our emotions. It lets us decide how we want to respond, rather than just react. I recently dealt with a complaint by reaction – I was professional enough but, on reflection, I realised it was not in line with my values. I wasn't able to change my response on that occasion, but I did take the time to rewrite a much better response, which is now saved in my files as a template for handling future complaints.

The same goes for the conversation we have with ourselves – in our own heads. I know my inner critic is far harsher when I'm rushing against the clock. When I slow down, I'm much kinder, much more reasonable and much more inspired, too.

Creativity

We are human beings, not robots. Our productivity doesn't just depend on speed and efficiency. It also depends on our creativity, our intuition and our innovation, and these things need space to flourish. Nothing shuts down inspiration faster than forcing it. In fact, sometimes when I'm really stuck I find taking the pressure off can be just the thing to get my creativity flowing.

I recently admitted to another writer that I sometimes reread my own writing – pieces that I feel particularly proud of. It feels completely indulgent, embarrassingly egotistic and highly unproductive, but my friend reminded me that I was simply immersing myself in my art. And if that fuels my creativity, it's actually highly productive.

Stress

Manically rushing from one thing to another is no good for your health or your productivity. Yes, a certain level of adrenaline can be really useful to beat inertia and fire up motivation, but when our stress levels get too high we make mistakes and poor decisions, we misjudge and misread situations and are far more likely to get caught up in reactive firefighting rather than productively moving forwards with what really matters.

The very act of slowing down can physically reduce our stress levels. Next time you find yourself feeling stressed or rushed, deliberately slow yourself down. Walk slower, talk slower, take slower, deeper breaths and notice the clarity of thought returning.

Happiness

Some of the best moments in life are ones we can't plan for. When we rush from one thing to another or pack things in too tightly, we can miss those moments: a conversation with a really friendly taxi driver; the moment when your daughter wants to have a long sleepy chat about dolphins; the statue you walk past every day and never really stop to see that it's carved out of a tree.

Take holidays, for example. It's not the ones that have a packed itinerary that stand out the most. The most memorable ones for me are slow days. Sitting in my dad's garden reading a book while my children watered flowers, picked berries and fed fish. Blowing bubbles by a lake. Running for an hour – simply because I felt like it – and I didn't have to rush back for a certain time. Even my children's most magical memories are more likely to involve hours of jumping on a trampoline rather than hours of queuing at theme parks.

In a world where time is precious, let's not forget to take our time. Enjoy the time that we do have. Let's not get caught up in doing everything faster and more efficiently. Sometimes work is better and life is richer when we take the time to slow down.

Release the breaks

Having said all that, going slowly doesn't always make things easier.

I was chatting to a lovely virtual assistant, who said that she knows she has capacity for more clients when she finds herself taking longer to do everything. She finds herself procrastinating, idling, skirting around decisions, spending all morning doing something that, frankly, would take only 20 minutes if the heat was on. She was craving the deadlines, the urgency, the challenge of juggling multiple commitments and clients asking her to bail them out of a tight spot at the last minute.

Having just spent several days with another client who was feeling quite the opposite, this made me smile. I wonder if we each have an optimum speed at which we do our best work – when we get our best output, satisfaction and enjoyment from our work?

When we're going too fast, it becomes overwhelming, unsustainable and unenjoyable, but when we're going too slowly, well that's hard work too. Like a car that's stuck in between gears: going slightly too fast for one gear, but not quite fast enough for the next. The revs are a bit too high, the engine is chugging away and it's an uncomfortable ride. It takes effort to keep going at that pace, and probably more fuel, rather than putting your foot down a little bit more and taking it up a gear so you can cruise along.

Going too slow can be lethargic and draining. It can take more effort to get started and keep going – like trying to start a weak car battery on a cold day. It can be deceptive and distracting: as soon as you think you've got plenty of time, it's too easy to notice the endless world of shiny things, little jobs, nags and thoughts of, 'I'll just...' Going too slow can also keep you in zombie mode, where you don't feel up to doing anything creative, complex or outside your comfort zone, stealing your motivation, confidence and decisiveness.

Speed up

If you feel stuck in a place where you are going too slow, perhaps it's time to step up a gear. Challenge yourself. What if you could get your work done in three days instead of five? Parkinson's Law states that work expands to fill the time available, so why not set yourself a deadline and see if you can rise to the challenge?

IT business consultant Richard Tubb decided to experiment with working a four-day working week. Once he'd made the commitment to take Fridays off he found that with some adjustment, he fitted into a four-day working week rhythm and now gets his work done in the time he has available and has Fridays free for other pursuits.

What if your day was done in six hours instead of eight? What would you love to do with the other two? Take on a new project, ramp up your business or start that ambitious thing you keep putting off? Do something fun, see someone you've been meaning to see for ages or do something wholly and wholeheartedly good for you?

What's your optimum speed?

Where do you need to slow down? Where could you do with speeding up? How might you play with your speed? As human beings, we have the capacity to operate at a spectrum of speeds: when we put our minds to it, we can run faster than we ever imagined and, when we choose to, we can deliberately slow down and drink in life. And, let's face it, life and work are certainly more interesting when we mix it up a bit.

Work–life rhythm: a working guide

I haven't had a 9–5 job for a long time. Ever since I became a mum nine years ago, I've been juggling and experimenting with different working patterns – from two mornings to three days a week, evenings, weekends, random nap times and varying combinations of nursery, childminders and amazing, supportive friends.

I never knew how to answer the question 'how many hours a week do you work?' because every week was different. When my youngest started school last September, I found myself with five days a week to work again. And this, too, has been an experiment.

There have been short days, where I find myself saying: 'What? 3 o'clock already?!' to crazy long days. There have been indulgent days off where I've run off to spend a day at a spa with my best friend with no phone signal (because, if I don't make these things happen, they never just happen), as well as slightly random days where I've woken insanely early for meetings, written three articles then gone on an Easter egg hunt, watched an egg and spoon race and watched both my children perform on stage – one as a chicken, the other in *The Tempest*.

It doesn't always work out, at least not the way I planned, and I've had some interesting lessons in saying no – including once turning down an opportunity to work with Hugh Grant – and instead saying yes to what really mattered to me, like the day I did a workshop first thing in Birmingham, came back to Stafford to watch Punch and Judy and eat ice cream with my daughter to celebrate the end of her reception year at school, before jumping on another train to London.

Some friends think I'm crazy. 'What a nightmare!' said one of my colleagues. But, on the contrary, it's my dream in progress. As I told them, I wouldn't have it any other way. I get to do work I love, with people I love working with, and be there for the people I love. Yes, it's hard work, yes, it's a juggle, yes, it's messy.

And no, I wouldn't call it balanced at all. And that's ok because I've never really believed in balance. Instead, I've been learning to find my own rhythm. And it's most definitely an ongoing experiment. But here's what I've learned so far:

- There will be highs and lows, ebb and flow. Life is not uniform, so don't try and make it that way. Generally speaking, flat lines usually indicate an absence of life.

- Allow yourself to run with life when it speeds up and you'll realise you can indeed run. You might even find it addictive – don't say I didn't warn you!

- Create pauses. Don't wait for the music to stop. Be deliberate about creating moments to stop, pause, take a deep breath, recover and recharge.

- A steady beat holds everything together. Develop habits and structure to give yourself some constant.

- Don't try to work out all the steps before you start. The only way to find your groove is to start moving.

- Learn to speed up and slow down. There is beauty and brilliance in both. Much of my learning this year has been in soaking in the slow moments as well as enjoying the thrill of the rollercoaster. Don't wish any of it away.

- There's a season for everything. Whatever you choose to do with each moment, do it wholeheartedly.

- There is life at work and life outside of work. Don't forget to live it.

- Play with your rhythm. Make it up as you go along. Sometimes you'll fall, sometimes you'll fly.

- Everything is negotiable. It's ok to create your own rules.

Over to you

Work and life

How much flexibility do I have? What opportunities and challenges does this flexibility give me?

....

....

Where do I need to set my own finish lines?

....

....

How's my work-life integrity? Am I the same person at work and outside of work?

....

....

How's my quality of life at work and outside of work? What one action can I take to improve it?

....

How's my work-life rhythm? How would I like it to be?

....

Daily rhythms

When are my best times? What's the most appropriate thing to do in those times?

....

....

Three things that would help me to start the day well are:

1. ....

2. ....

3. ....

Work that energises me:

....

....

....

Work that drains me:

....

....

....

How wobbly is my line?

....

My recovery strategy

Five things that help me to refuel, recharge and recover my energy are:

1. ....
2. ....
3. ....
4. ....
5. ....

Playing with my speed

Two ways I can experiment with slowing down are:

1. ....
2. ....

Two ways I can experiment with speeding up are:

1. ....
2. ....

Chapter 9

Jumping off the guilt trip

S tress and guilt often are the symptoms that drive us to improve our productivity, but a life driven by stress and guilt is not a brilliant or productive one. This chapter lifts the lid on how these factors actually affect our productivity and how to change the way we respond in order to put ourselves back in the driving seat.

Is guilt stealing your time?

In the quest for productivity, we talk a lot about time, organisation, tools, schedules, techniques, emails, distraction, interruptions, motivation, mindset, vision, action, procrastination, deadlines and focus.

But there's something I often hear, that none of us explicitly talks about. I hear it hiding in the frustration of not being able to say no and the exhaustion of sacrificing sleep for the sake of catching up. I hear it lurking in the resignation of 'I'd love to, but...' and 'if only I had more time'. I hear it prowling in the pressure of trying to keep on top of everything, the worry of letting someone down, the struggle of trying – and failing – to please everyone and get everything done.

That thing is guilt.

> 'I feel guilty when I'm working and not there for my kids... and when I'm with my kids and not working.'

> 'I feel guilty that I'm neglecting my health, but also when I take time off for me.'

> 'I feel guilty when I have to work late... and when I leave the office.'

> 'I feel guilty when I'm on holiday... and I know I'm guilty of not taking enough time off.'

> 'I wake up guilty knowing that there are emails waiting for me on my Blackberry.'

Guilt shows up everywhere.

It shows up when we're working and when we're not working; when we show up, when we switch off; when we bring work home and when we leave work undone; when we miss out on school plays, sports days and bedtimes, as well as when we take time off for our children, for sick days and school strikes; when we forget birthdays and miss deadlines, but also when we can't forget about work.

And its constant message is this: 'You don't have enough time. You're not doing enough.' Some of us even use guilt to spur us on, to tell ourselves and others: 'You have to do more.'

But what does guilt actually do?

Guilt distracts us

Ever notice how the thing you feel guilty about is never the thing you are focused on? When you're working, guilt tells you that you're neglecting your family, your health, your house or your relationships. When you are not working, guilt taps you on the shoulder and reminds you of the email you forgot to send or the meeting you are not preparing for.

Guilt thrives on counting losses: all the things you've missed, not done or are not doing right now. Forget the lovely Sunday afternoon you have just had with your kids and count the seconds you're not spending with them. Forget the magical moment you just had when he took off on his bike without you holding on, and keep beating yourself up about the first step you missed when you were at work. Forget the brilliant victory you have just pulled out of the bag at work, and keep counting the jobs that are still on your to-do list.

By default, guilt distracts and diminishes our capacity. Just like when we try to drive in one direction while looking in another, or a child starts running one way while looking somewhere else; it's exhausting, ineffective and, frankly, a disaster waiting to happen. You cannot pay full attention to something if you're constantly looking over your shoulder, and guilt always draws our attention to what we are not doing.

Guilt devalues our time

Research from Stanford University Graduate School of Business suggests that people who are time-affluent, who feel like they have more time, are people who regularly experience a sense of awe, being captivated by the present moment.[1]

Guilt, on the other hand, steals our ability to be in the present. Instead of enjoying the time that we do have, we end up worrying about what we don't have time for, what's not been done and what's not gone well. Instead of giving ourselves permission to be completely absorbed in the moment, to fully experience what's right in front of us, guilt whisks us away – our bodies might be present, but our minds start time travelling – replaying past regrets and fretting about the future.

Worrying itself takes time, energy and attention. As cricketer Glenn Turner put it:

> **'Worrying is like a rocking chair, it gives you something to do, but it gets you nowhere.'**

The more we worry about not having enough time, the less time we seem to have.

Guilt disables us

What have you told yourself you'd love to do someday, when you have time? What do you find yourself saying you'd love to do 'if only you had the time'? What do you keep putting off, waiting for that elusive moment when everything else is done and you finally 'have time'?

Guilt holds us back from pursuing the things that really matter to us – the bold business idea or brave career move, the trip you've always wanted to make or the book you keep meaning to write, the stuff that matters to you, that perhaps nobody else is ever going to chase you up on.

Take the rocking chair test: imagine yourself aged 96, looking back on your life – what would you be most proud of? What would you consider to have been time well spent? Chances are those are precisely the things that guilt tells us we don't have time for.

Not enough time

Guilt has a way of sneaking in and making itself at home. Somewhere along the line, we've accepted guilt as a permanent resident in our lives – sitting on our shoulder, at the dinner table, in the bath with our kids... and its constant message is 'not enough'. There's not enough time. You're not doing enough. You're not enough. The guilt-driven life is one of fear, where nothing is ever enough.

Guilt has us believing that we don't have enough time, but what if guilt is the very thing that's stealing our time? What if we stopped feeling guilty about our time? What if we said no to guilt?

What if we said *enough*?

Enough with the guilt trip. Enough with the exhausting cycle of never having, doing or being enough. Because, quite frankly, that's not working. Let's redefine our relationship with time. Let's start a new conversation about time. Let's ditch the guilt and start telling the truth about time.

Guilt tells us there is never enough. So, let's start with enough. Instead of what we don't have time for, let's start talking about what we do have time for. Let's start with what we do have and what we are doing. Let's celebrate that and start from there.

When you start from enough, you stop getting distracted by trying to find more and you make the most of what you do have. How much time do you have: 10 minutes, 10 days, 10 months? Instead of wishing you had more, focus on what you do have and what you're going to do with it.

When you start from enough, you appreciate what you have; you value it, love it, treasure it, enjoy it, instead of worrying about where the next thing is going to come from. Not sure how everything's going to play out next week? That's ok, you'll work it out. But if now is not the moment to figure it out, then let it go. Focus on the person, the moment or the fork-ful of food that's right in front of you right now and enjoy it.

When you start from enough you stop holding yourself back and you actually start. And you know that's where the magic happens. It's from a place of enough that we grow and create more. So, I'll start with this:

You have enough. You do enough. You are enough.

Now, what are you going to do with that?

How to feel like you have more time

In 2012, psychological scientists Melanie Rudd, Jennifer Aaker and Kathleen Vohs embarked on a study to understand what makes people feel like they have more time and what makes some people time-rich, when others feel time-poor.[2]

They studied awe – the experience of being captivated by the present moment –

> 'whether it's the breathtaking scope of the Grand Canyon, the ethereal beauty of the Aurora Borealis, or the exhilarating view from the top of the Eiffel Tower – at some point in our lives we've all had the feeling of being in a complete and overwhelming sense of awe'.[3]

They found that awe changes our subjective experience of time. It makes time slow down – not the actual ticking of the seconds, but in how we experience it. It expands our perception of time.

> 'When you feel awe, you feel very present – it captivates you in the current moment,' says Rudd. 'And when you are so focused on the here and now, the present moment is expanded – and time along with it.'[4]

This certainly chimes with Gay Hendrick's theory of Einstein Time (time is relative) versus Newtonian Time (time is finite) in his book *The Big Leap*. An hour with your beloved feels like a minute; a minute on a hot stove feels like an hour. Depending on what we do, space seems to narrow or to expand, time seems to slow down or accelerate.

As one Head of Talent put it:

> 'I work 8 to 5 with half an hour for lunch and because it's my bliss it feels like about 2 hours. Time is weird.'

Awe also makes us feel like we have more time available. We become more patient and less materialistic and more willing to volunteer our time to help other people. People who feel like they have more time are more generous with their time and experience greater life satisfaction, too:

> 'Experiences of awe bring people into the present moment, and being in the present moment underlies awe's capacity to adjust time perception, influence decisions, and make life feel more satisfying than it would otherwise.'[5]

Magic moments

How easy is it to generate awe? Do you have to travel to the Grand Canyon or Paris? Or might these moments be found a bit closer to home, too?

Perhaps it is the feeling of being beautifully overwhelmed by a sunset or a stranger's generosity. Or being completely lost in a book, a work of art or a hot bubble bath. Or those goosebump moments when life surprises and delights you.

Here's an experiment – start noticing your magic moments and let yourself be captivated by them. Then capture them – write them down or tell someone else. I have one client who has cultivated a habit of capturing his AMGLs: achievements, magic moments, gratitudes and learning moments. Writing them in a notebook roughly once a month, he now has five years' worth of these to look back on.

What might your moments of awe be? Whatever they are, when we allow ourselves to be captivated by the present moment, we'll feel like we have all the time in the world.

Daily treasures

There's a lovely old man who comes into my writing cave – the local café where I'm fast becoming part of the furniture as I write this book. He's a regular, too – he usually visits as part of his daily routine to get out of the house, pick up a couple of things from M&S, then stop by the café to read his paper over a cup of coffee and usually a few extra treats from the staff.

He used to volunteer at another café (I seem to live my life in cafés!) where I used to take my children, and has known them since they were babies. Normally we say hello, he asks about my family and he settles down to his coffee and paper while I carry on typing.

On Good Friday, however, the café was busy. I had negotiated a few precious hours to type away in my little corner when I spotted him come in and turn around, and his face fell as he noticed there were no free tables. Despite the staff calling out to him to wait, he said he'd come back tomorrow. I called out to him and he looked in my direction without seeing me, his eyes dejected and his shoulders slumped.

I ran after him. I had to, to invite him to share my table (he would say I attacked him).

'Are you sure I won't be bothering you? Haven't you got work to do?' he asked.

I wouldn't take no for an answer.

We talked for ages – about his life, his family, his memories. Memories he hadn't visited for a long time, stories that came pouring out because there was somebody to hear them. I learned more about this man in a couple of hours than in some six years of knowing him.

'You've really made my Easter weekend', he told me, 'with all these memories fresh in my mind.'

'Aren't I boring you?' he kept asking.

'Not at all.' I replied.

He kept apologising for taking up my time and kept wondering, suspiciously, if I was a good listener or a good actress.

'Haven't you got work to do?'

Yes, about 30,000 words' worth. But that didn't matter right then. Right then I got to watch this man come alive, as he relived perfectly ordinary memories that meant the world to him. I got to watch the sparkle come back to his eyes, his shoulders bounce as he laughed, his face light up as the joy of those moments poured into the present.

He refused to leave without buying me lunch. So I made him a deal – if he was to buy me lunch, then he wasn't allowed to feel guilty for 'taking my time'. Because it was a pleasure and a privilege, it really was. To see him come alive, to know that, in that moment, whatever I had planned, whatever I had on my list, right there and then I was in absolutely the right place, doing absolutely the right thing. And all I had to do was sit and listen.

And that was his gift to me. To be fully in the moment, witnessing this man recall moments past with a joy that was so tangible and present – because he was fully present in the moment when he first experienced them. That's the gift of being in the moment. When you live fully in the moment, you get to relive it, time and time again.

Stress

Stress has become commonplace in our working lives (and, arguably, every other part of our lives, too!). We experience stress when there's too much work, when there's not enough work, when everything happens at once and when nothing seems to be happening. We get stressed about the demands other people have of us – and the expectations we place on ourselves. We can experience stress over a wide range of situations, from the state of the economy or the environment, to finding socks, parking spaces and grey hairs. 'I'm stressed' has become part of everyday vocabulary, even among school children.

What actually happens when we get stressed? And is it always a bad thing?

Psychologist Rob Archer suggests that 'human beings are well evolved to deal with acute stress, but less well evolved to deal with chronic stress'.

Acute stress happens when something puts immediate pressure on us to act, like being chased by a lion. The human stress response primes our bodies to move quickly to stay alive: our attention span narrows, giving us extreme focus on one thing, energy is diverted away from less imme- diately essential systems, such as our immune or digestive systems, to our big muscles (so that we can run and stay alive!).

Of course, for most of us our stresses are likely to be psychological rather than facing actual lions. As human beings we have the capacity to create stress any time we like: when we have a difficult conversation, a big decision to make, changes to navigate or deadlines to meet. The acute stress response can actually be quite useful: when we are firefighting an emergency or working to a tight deadline, energy to move and increased focus is not a bad thing to have at all.

The problem comes when acute stress becomes chronic stress. When there are five different emergencies all crying out for our attention, we become overwhelmed and lose our focus. When our energy becomes depleted because we are constantly in emergency mode, we become exhausted. When our digestive and immune systems have been shut down for too long, our health suffers. As human beings we're probably never going to be caught by a lion, but we can be caught by fatigue.

The answer isn't to avoid stress. As Rob Archer explains:

> **'If I care about something, I will stress about it. To avoid a life of stress would be to avoid a life of meaning. What we need to do is make sure that the stress we experience is in service of the things we care about – and that we are strategic about how we spend and recover our energy.'**

Stanford University psychologist Kelly McGonigal also suggests that how we think about our stress also changes its impact on our health. One study found that people who experienced a lot of stress – and believed that stress is harmful for your health – had a 43-per-cent increased risk of dying. People who experienced a lot of stress but didn't view stress as harmful actually had the lowest risk of dying of anyone in the study, including people who had relatively little stress.

In her TED Talk, 'How to Make Stress Your Friend'[6], Kelly McGonigal explains that:

> **'When you change your mind about stress, you can change your body's response to stress.'**

Instead of seeing stress as harmful, she suggested seeing the stress response as a sign that your body is energised and preparing you to meet a challenge. The image that comes to my mind is one of an athlete about to start a race.

One of the acute responses to stress is that our heart rate goes up and our breathing increases to deliver more oxygen to our brain. In a typical stress response, when our heart rate goes up, our blood vessels constrict, which is one of the reasons that chronic stress is sometimes associated with cardiovascular disease. However, McGonigal found that when participants viewed their stress response as helpful for their performance, they were less anxious and more confident, their heart was still pounding but their blood vessels stayed relaxed: 'It actually looks a lot like what happens in moments of joy and courage.'

How could you use the energy created by stress, if you choose to see it differently?

What are your feelings trying to tell you?

It's always good to check and challenge our feelings. As a friend once said to me, 'Sometimes I need to remind myself that, just because I'm in a bad mood, doesn't mean I have a bad life.' Sometimes it can also be useful not to dismiss our feelings or to try and get rid of a bad mood too quickly, but to dig a little deeper into our feelings of guilt and stress and pay attention to what they might be trying to tell us.

Stress, guilt and frustration can be a sign that something is out of kilter with our values, beliefs or expectations. Sometimes those expectations are wildly unrealistic (I must be all things to all people and get everything right) and lead to the constant guilt that just makes us feel terrible, but sometimes our feelings can serve us if we use them to help us to put a finger on something specific we want to change or do differently.

1. **Check your feelings.** What's behind this feeling? What thoughts, worries, or fears are creating this feeling of guilt, stress, frustration

or being overwhelmed? What do you believe to be true about this situation?

2. **Challenge your thinking.** Ask yourself, 'How true is that, really?'. How true is that underlying belief that emails need to be answered immediately, that your boss is out to get you, or that every moment you are not with your children you are neglecting them? Sometimes our feelings can come from underlying beliefs that are based on past truths, part truths or pure imagination.

3. **Clarify what's important.** Rather than focusing on the fear or worry itself, what is it that you value that feels threatened here? Get to the core of what's important, so you can focus on making changes that honour what you do want, rather than react to what you don't want.

4. **Change your perspective.** What's another way to look at this? What are the positives? What else is going on or going well? Do you see a heavy schedule or a week full of opportunities? Pressure to perform or the opportunity to do your best work? Curveballs or plot twists? Failure or the opportunity to do something new? Doors closing or new beginnings? Chaos or beauty in formation? Perspective matters. What you see shapes your world and how you live in it.

5. **Choose your response.** What can you do differently? What positive changes can you make? What actions can you take that will help you to honour what's important?

Reclaiming good

Sometimes, the pursuit of achievement and greatness can leave us feeling inadequate, exhausted and underwhelmed. Sometimes we can be so consumed with achieving more, we can forget to enjoy what we have and what is good.

In his book *The Artisan Soul*, Erwin McManus says this:

> 'There's a subtle side effect when it comes to the language of *good* and *great*. *Good* has become less than *great*. *Good* has become *above average*. *Good to great* has become the same as *better to*

best, when in fact they are of different qualities altogether when it comes to essence... Great is about execution and achievement, good is about essence and ethos. The artisan soul aspires to do great work but never neglects the importance of being inspired by all that's good and beautiful.'

Often we associate productivity with greatness – the act of doing more, achieving goals and reaching upwards and outwards, but I think true productivity is also about goodness. It's about doing good work, beautiful work, satisfying work. It's about living a good life – one where we embrace and enjoy being as much as becoming. Where exploring, wondering (and wandering) and asking questions are just as valid as achieving, reaching and having answers.

Over to you

How much does guilt distract me, disable me or devalue my time?

....

What would I do differently if I started with enough? *I have enough. I do enough. I am enough.*

....

What would I love to do one day, when I have time?

....

What am I most proud of?

....

What do I consider time well spent?

....

Some of my recent magic moments or experiences of awe are:

....

....

My plan to capture and create more of these is:

....

....

What do I get stressed about? Is it in service of something I care about?

....

How can I use the energy created by stress? Stress can be of use to me when:

....

When I'm in emergency mode, am I focused on one emergency or several emergencies?

....

....

....

....

....

How strategic am I about recovering? Do I give myself time to recharge?

....

....

....

....

....

When I feel stressed I choose to:

....

....

....

....

....

My definition of good work is:

....

....

....

....

....

Chapter 10

The art of juggling

Life is messy and complicated. It's not just at work where we want to feel more in control, fulfilled and productive, but in all aspects of our lives – our family life, home, personal goals, community projects, voluntary work, hobbies, social life. Different roles, multiple projects and competing priorities in our work and personal life rarely form an orderly queue and wait for our attention (as much as we would like them to).

Do you multitask or compartmentalise? Do you do it all yourself or do you ask for help? Juggling is something we all have to do, so let's explore what it takes for you to juggle all that's important to you.

Multitasking: magic or myth?

Multitasking. Some people love it, others hate it. Some see it as necessity, given the multiple roles, responsibilities, commitments and projects we juggle. But does it actually work?

First things first, multitasking is not actually multitasking. When we try and perform two tasks simultaneously, what we're really doing is switching and rapidly refocusing between tasks, and while it might feel productive, each switch costs us in time, attention and productivity – sometimes just a few tenths of a seconds, sometimes much more. (Remember the Microsoft experiment? 1 minute interruption = average 15-minute recovery?) This is especially true when we're repeatedly switching back and forth between tasks. Research suggests that even brief mental blocks created by shifting between tasks can cost as much as 40 per cent of your productive time.[1]

Something I spotted on Twitter a while ago often rings a bell: 'I feel like I have too many tabs open in my head!' Every time I mention it in a talk or a workshop, I see eyes light up and heads nodding furiously: 'Yes, that's exactly how I feel!'. What happens when we've got too many tabs open on our computer? It slows down, crashes or stops working. It's also easier to get distracted when we're clicking between tabs – to accidentally click on the wrong tab or let something shiny catch our eye and end up going off on a tangent. Have you ever been closing down your tabs and windows at the end of the day, only to find that one email you forgot to press send on first thing in the morning?

It's much easier to make mistakes when we're multitasking. A few years ago I was writing Christmas cards while Catherine, my very excited three-year-old, was asking me repeatedly, 'Is it Christmas yet, Mummy? Is it Christmas yet, Mummy? Is it Christmas yet, Mummy?' with the unwavering enthusiasm, energy and volume that only a three-year-old has – and I found myself signing off one card with 'Lots of love, Grante, Grace, Oliver and Christmas'. It's not hard to write a Christmas card! But it's very easy to make a mistake when you are switching your focus between different things.

Have you ever sent an email to the wrong person? Or, worse, sent it to the person you were talking about rather than the person you wanted to talk to? One workshop delegate I worked with once responded to this question with 'Um... we don't talk about that.' Oops.

The worst multitasking mistake I've come across so far is the case of Tomasz Paczkowski, a man who, in trying to prove a point to his wife, decided to multitask by doing the ironing while watching TV and drinking a beer at the same time. It was all going well until he got so involved in the boxing on the TV that, when the phone rang, he picked up the iron and pressed it to his ear. Ouch! So, multitasking can be bad for your health as well as your productivity!

If you came to my house at breakfast time, you might argue that multitasking is a necessity but, believe me, it doesn't take much – one spilt drink, one squabble, one child suddenly remembering they're supposed to be wearing something blue that day – for me to burn the toast or put the dishwasher tablet in the coffee. So, yes, sometimes the world doesn't form an orderly queue to wait for our full attention and we do have to juggle multiple tasks from time to time, but be aware that when your attention is split, nothing is getting your full and best attention. Give yourself a break and don't throw in any more balls to juggle than you have to.

Is there ever a good time to multitask?

There are times when I find splitting my attention can be quite useful. When I'm running, I like to listen to a podcast or catch up on a talk, because it helps to take my mind off my aching legs. Lately I've taken to running with a friend, and we've found that it's a great way to catch up and have a natter while getting fit, and it saves us cash and calories from the coffee and cake we'd be having otherwise. Plus, there's an added bonus of the accountability you get when you know that someone's going to be knocking on your door at 7 am to go for that run.

Other ways of killing two birds with one stone can include:

- walking meetings

- breakfast or lunch meetings (although don't give up all your breaks this way!)

- arranging to meet someone at an event or immediately before/after to cut down on travelling

- car sharing or travelling to an event together

- reading a book on the train

- listening to audio books while commuting

- watching a video while on the treadmill (**only** on a treadmill; this doesn't work on the road!)

- recording a conversation or talk and having it transcribed for an article

- taking your ideas into the bath – and keeping bath crayons handy to capture any bright ideas (a friend of mine uses eyeliner to write on the tiles, but that seems a bit expensive to me!)

- turning chores into activities for the children (oh, just me?)

- batching 'out and about' errands to complete together (e.g., buying stamps for work and a birthday card for your mum or posting something you sold on eBay at the same time as your latest customer samples)

- business meetings in play areas when all parties are juggling childcare – I wouldn't recommend it for all occasions, but there was a time when I used to run child-friendly networking meetings where our kids played in the same room, and I also held a coaching session once with a client on a beach while our children entertained themselves happily by the water, and I'm pretty sure the scenery did us good too!

Compartmentalising: also sounds better than it works!

THE ART OF JUGGLING

While my natural tendency is to take on too much and try and do too many things together, my husband goes the other way. If he had his way, life would be neatly compartmentalised into separate areas: family, work, study, friends, house, health (and probably gadgets would have its own compartment, too), where everything has its place and time and could be balanced. That way he would always know where he stood, what mode or role he needed to be in and where his priority and focus was at any given time.

Unfortunately for him, life doesn't really work like that either. We made the decision for him to take a sabbatical from work this year so that he could do his Master's degree full time, because we knew that trying to juggle part-time study, full-time work and family commitments would just be hell for him. Even so, he still finds studying with family commitments hard.

It's not just the time he spends at lectures, it's the reading, research, essays and projects that need to be completed in between. Even when the children are at school and I'm working away, he says he's still not able to completely switch off family and bury himself in study, as mentally he's still on standby in case the school calls.

Sometimes life is messier than we would like. Children get ill. Global conference calls, travel or a work crisis might call on you outside of normal office hours. Different areas of our lives cross over and overlap and sometimes that's a good thing: a work contact you call on in your school governor position or a lesson learned in parenting that applies equally well to contract negotiations. When the different facets of our lives work well together, they enhance each other. Being good at what I do, being on fire and on purpose at work, makes me a better parent. And I can't count the number of productivity lessons I've learned from being a parent. As Anne-Marie Slaughter said in her TED talk:[2]

> '**When family comes first, work doesn't come second. Life comes together.**'

I'm often asked in workshops if I would recommend having separate diaries, to-do lists and 'second brain' systems for work and home life. My answer is this: we take the same brain to work as we do to home. So it's natural that ideas, nags and reminders may come up at work that need dealing with at home, and vice versa. It may or may not be appropriate to deal with at work in that moment, but if we carry it around in our heads until we get home, it takes up even more headspace while we're at work. Sometimes a home-related thing just might be simpler to deal with in the working day – for example, calls that need to be made during office hours or asking a colleague where he takes his son to play cricket. And, sometimes, home-related things might get triggered off at work – for example, when I get a workshop booking that requires some travel, I might need to make childcare arrangements and discuss logistics with my husband. Being able to access my second brain right there and then and park it in my @home or @grante category means that I can forget about it until I'm in the right context to deal with it later.

Doing it all or doing your all?

The secret to having and doing it all is in the word 'all'.

It brings out the perfectionist in us. As a new mum, my idea of motherhood was a collection of the best traits I admired in all the mothers I had ever known. Some were amazing cooks, some had the patience of a saint, some were super organised, some looked stunning, some had great careers, some could play with children for hours on end... and I tried to live up to all of those things and more – something that's just not meant for one person to be. No wonder I never measured up.

Equally, it's easy to look at an array of successful businesses and see excellence in every field – those who have a creative genius about them, those with killer instincts and impeccable timing, those who could sell snow to the Eskimos, those who are great with numbers, confident speakers, prolific writers, technical whizzes and strategic masterminds.

Each role we take on can have huge potential scope – think of all the different types of doctors there are. Can you imagine one person being an expert in every field of medicine and being able to serve people in all those areas? When there is no definition all definitions can apply, and we can find ourselves trying to fulfil a very wide range of expectations. Many of those can leave us feeling like a square peg in a round hole.

Having it all doesn't mean being everybody or doing everything. It's about being you with everything that you've got – whatever situation you're in. Rather than being all things to all people, productivity is as much about what you don't do as what you do do.

Who are you under all your hats? What makes you you? How would you play your roles differently from everyone else? Remember your strengths and preferences in Chapter 7 and your values in Chapter 1? Use these insights to help shape what your 'all' looks like.

Defining your all

If we are going to juggle, to play multiple roles in multiple arenas, we need to be deliberately selective about what each of those roles looks like – for us, personally. Not what it looks like for other people or for our predecessors. Not what it's always looked like, what others expect it to look like, or what it should look like. It's time to challenge the status quo, existing assumptions and redefine your role.

Just as specialising in a niche enables a business to be more focused, distinctive and profitable, defining your role will allow you to focus your efforts, to shine brightly rather than spread thinly and feel satisfied and fulfilled rather than have shoes so big that no one could ever fill them. The more tailored your role, the better you can fill it and find fulfilment in it.

Here's a quick 10-minute exercise you can use to begin to define your roles.

On a piece of paper, draw a 3×3 grid with nine boxes. In each of these boxes, write one of your roles, e.g. husband, accountant, writer, dad.

Now imagine you are at your own funeral and significant people are standing up to talk about you in each of these roles. Or, if that's too morbid, imagine you're a fly on the wall at a party and you overhear someone saying nice things about you behind your back. What would you want them to be saying about you? What would be the most meaningful compliment to you?

Back to that piece of paper: in each of the boxes, under each role, write the words 'I am' and fill in the word(s) that would most describe how you want to be in that role right now. Give yourself just a few seconds on each one and pick the strongest word that comes to mind quickly. This exercise works best when you don't overthink it.

MOTHER	WIFE	BUSINESS OWNER
I am...	I am...	I am...
WRITER	SPEAKER	RUNNER
MUSICIAN	FRIEND	DAUGHTER

Reflecting on what you've written, consider:

- When am I most like this? When am I not?

- Given what I've written here, what does success look like?

- What expectations, commitments or tolerations could I let go of to pursue this more freely?

- What's really important to me? What's not so important?

- What can only I do? What can be delegated, renegotiated or released?

- What do I need to focus on in this season?

Your roles pie

This is another more in-depth exercise I use with clients who are juggling multiple roles.

1. What are your different roles in life? (Choose eight.)

Some might be work-related, such as accountant, trainer or business director. Some might relate to personal relationships, such as friend, family member, partner, parent. Some might relate to hobbies, interests or personal development goals, such as runner, singer, speaker or chef. List them.

Makes sure you include 'me' as one of your eight roles – you need to be your own coach and caretaker as well.

Is there a fantasy role that you'd like to include? Something you've always wanted to do? For example, rally car racer, business owner or novelist.

You can have only eight roles, so if you have more than eight you might want to combine certain ones, e.g. sister, cousin, daughter might become family member, mountain climber, bungee jumper, and open-water swimmer might become adventurer.

1. Me (own coach/caretaker)
2. ....
3. ....
4. ....
5. ....
6. ....
7. ....
8. ....

Once you have decided on your eight roles, write them around a circle divided into eight segments.

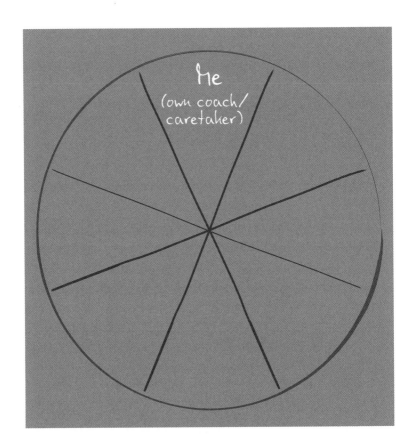

2. Where are you right now?

For each section, give yourself a score from 1–10 on how well you're performing in these roles right now, not compared to anyone else's standards
or expectations, but according to your own definition of success.

3. What does success look like?

For each role, what would a score of 10 look like? What would you like
to achieve? Why is that important to you?

4. What would a one-point improvement be? (For example, from
three to four or from seven to eight.)

5. What's your primary role for this current season?

What do you want to be paying particular attention to?

There are times when one role might take centre stage and the other roles might take more of a backstage – still important, but perhaps your focus in those areas might be to keep them nicely ticking over rather than go all out. Pursuing that CEO promotion, preparing for a wedding and training for your first marathon are all worthy goals, for example, but perhaps not ones you would want to pursue at exactly the same time. What takes centre stage right now?

Asking for help

There's a saying that really riles me:

> *'If it's to be, it's up to me.'*

I know, I know, it's meant to be empowering – to take action and responsibility, to take the reins and be in charge of your own life. But, too often, it gets interpreted as:

> *'Do it yourself. You're on your own.'*

When you're faced with challenges, when things don't work, when you're overwhelmed. When you have too many ideas, or not enough, and can't see the wood for the trees. When you have lost your mojo, when you are feeling terrible, when you are beating yourself up. When you can't remember your name, let alone what you're trying to achieve. When you are racing round like a headless chicken or when you're stuck.

> *Don't ask for help, don't collaborate, don't phone a friend. Go figure – it's up to you.*

Yes, it's up to you to take action – to take your own baby steps and big leaps of faith, to stretch outside your comfort zone, to grow and to be the change you want to see in your world. Self-sufficiency is a wonderful thing, but I prefer resourcefulness.

Being resourceful means you don't have to do it all yourself. You don't have to be good at everything. You have full permission to be brilliant at some things and hopeless at others – you choose what you put your energy into. You know who you are and who you are not and you're ok with that. You are not superwoman or superman – and that's a good thing. Resourcefulness means you ask for help and you learn from others. You build a superstar support team around you and you work with people who bring out the best in you.

> 'No one can whistle a symphony. It takes an orchestra to play it.'
>
> H. E. LUCCOCK, METHODIST MINISTER

No man or woman is an island. Over the years there have been many occasions where I had to get over myself and ask for help. Each time has proven to be a blessing – not just to me, but also to the person who was helping me. There is something very human and beautiful about admitting that you can't do everything, about shedding that superhero illusion and being open to asking for, and receiving, help. I truly believe that, as human beings, we're designed to live in community. That one person's pet hate truly can be someone else's joy. And when we step out of the way and let someone else fully step into their light, to do what they can do, what they love to do and what they do best, it's a blessing all round. When we allow ourselves to need each other, we open up the possibility of drawing the best out of each other.

Where do you need to ask for help?

Challenge your defaults

An article caught my eye recently. The first line asked 'Are you the default parent?', followed by 'If you have to think about it, you're not. You'd know. Trust me.' It gave a humorous and somewhat bleak account of all the things you scope, think about and are responsible for if you are the default parent.[3]

There were definitely parts I nodded furiously and laughed out loud at but I also realised there are times when I'm not the default parent. Like first thing in the morning, for example. If my daughter wakes up before I do (which she often does), Daddy is her go-to person because he's the morning person and is often awake or ready to wake when she comes in and she has learned that he's far more likely to respond to her requests for breakfast or to fix the TV than Mummy's slow and groggy 'in a minute', 'not now' and 'go back to bed' comments.

Equally, I'm not the parent who multitasks in the shower. I blatantly ignore my kids and they've learned that they won't get a sensible response out of Mummy until she's out of the shower. Kids will go to the person they're most likely to get a favourable response from. Daddy is the default hot-chocolate maker and sweets dispenser. Daddy is the one who does the funny voices with bedtime stories. But I am the default spider-catcher, the default clothes-drawer sorter, the default 'make me feel better' parent and definitely the person responsible for figuring out what's for tea.

What are you the default go-to person for – at work or at home? Here are some common examples:

The default oracle: the one who knows everything and everyone. The one people come to before they ask Google, Wiki, the intranet or the person who's actually responsible for answering that question.

The default fixer: the natural problem solver who is the first port of call when stuff hits the fan. The one who gets asked 'could you take a look at this' even when it's completely outside your area.

The default organiser: the one who takes the drinks order when you all rock up at a café and who has probably phoned ahead, booked the table in the corner and checked if there's soya milk for the dairy-intolerant person. The one everyone else turns to and asks 'What's the plan?'.

The default decision maker: the one who gets copied in on emails with 'What do you think?' and invited to meetings 'because we value your opinion'.

The default emergency hero: the one who you can always get hold of at the last minute, who you can rely upon to jump into action at the drop of a hat.

The default counsellor: The first person people turn to when they need a shoulder to cry on or a sounding board to rant at. The one who knows about all the make-ups and break-ups in the office, the hospital visits and whose children are teething.

The default perfecter: one person I worked with recently said that her perfectionism became so well known within her team, that someone she delegated to actually delivered the piece of work to her with the words: 'it's not quite there yet but I know you'll check it through and make it right'.

We choose our defaults, however much it feels the other way: sometimes deliberately because, actually, we quite like being that person (I'm really not that scared of spiders and I do enjoy cooking); sometimes because we made a decision once upon a time, when it made perfect sense, and haven't questioned it since. And others, well we just kind of fell into the habit.

It's good to revisit our defaults from time to time and to ask how well they're working for us. For example, while my husband is a full-time Master's student and I'm the one bringing home the bacon, should I be the default one to cook it too? The truth is I enjoy cooking so, unless I physically can't be there to do it, I tend to assume the responsibility. But if I'm starting to resent that, I need to be the one to change it.

How do you stop being the default person – if you choose to?

1. **Make yourself less available.** People will always default to the quickest or easiest route, so making it harder to find it from you can make all the other options far more attractive. Delay responding, be less accommodating, say no from time to time. Point them in the right direction, even if it takes just as much time as giving them the answer or doing it for them. Give them an incentive to go and find the answer by a different means.

2. **Hand over the responsibility.** I have a horrible habit of being indecisive and, sometimes, I'm guilty of asking others for their opinion, just to check and, essentially, to make my decision for me. Chief Ninja, Graham has pulled me up on this before and asked, 'Why did you need to check with me?' At other times, he has turned around and told me, 'You decide. I trust you.' Yes, in the same amount of time he could have made the decision for me, but this way he's training me to let go of using him as my crutch and get used to making my own decisions.

3. **Accept it takes time to learn.** My husband is a great cook, but he hasn't been the one to make sure dinner is on the table day in, day out for the last 12 years. So of course it's going to take him time to learn, to get used to it. And he probably won't do it the same way I did. He will need to figure out his own way of doing things and I need to let him. That's my learning curve, too. In fact, when I did finally hand over the

reins in the kitchen, his words were, 'I'll do it, as long as you leave me to it!' No feedback or help, no 'let me just show you'. That told me!

4. **Let it go.** As well as letting go of control, I also need to let go of being the default person. There's a part of me that likes being the default person, to be wanted and in demand. Honestly, that's probably the hardest part to let go of – my ego. I distinctly remember sitting upstairs one day, working on this book while my husband was cooking one of my signature stir-fry dishes for tea, realising I could choose to feel redundant or free to write – and it was scary how tempting it was to choose to be needed.

'Step away from the kitchen and enjoy every moment!' a Facebook friend reminded me.

What defaults do you need to step away from, so you can enjoy what you do more fully?

The art of juggling

A while ago I took a crash course in juggling. I had somehow been roped in to helping out with some children's work, and learning circus skills was one of the things I had to do. Interestingly, I was incredibly bad at juggling actual balls and spinning real plates! But one thing I noticed was this: even when you're juggling, you don't do everything at once.

You move one ball at a time. You get one up in the air before you move on to the next one. You release a ball before you catch another one. Successful jugglers don't throw all their balls in the air and hope to catch them all (even if some of them look like they're doing that for effect). The same goes for juggling life. If I try and pay attention to everything all at once, it's chaos. When I get one thing in motion first, I can then let it go and move on to the next thing. I can have different plates spinning, but only if I get them going one at a time. It's like cooking a roast dinner: you don't cook the chicken to perfection, then start peeling the potatoes, but equally you don't try and baste the chicken and peel the potatoes at the same time. You're cooking several things in tandem, but paying attention to each thing in turn.

Juggling takes practice. When you first start it's hard enough to juggle two items, but as you become more practised and the movement becomes familiar to your muscles, you find that certain moves become habit and you're able to take on more adventurous challenges. The things you're familiar with require less mental investment, and once you crack the basics, there's room to progress with less frustration.

There are certain things you can probably juggle in your sleep because you're so used to doing them, but new horizons and unfamiliar situations take time, attention and energy to get used to. A new job, becoming a parent, entering a new season in life or stepping into new territory all come with a learning curve. Every move needs attention. Every step we take, we're learning. And the chances are we'll get it wrong plenty of times before we get it right. As I learned in my early days of parenting, even when we do get it right another change can change what right looks like. And that's ok: life is something we make up as we go along.

Trying and failing is how you learn. A friend of mine, who runs workshops that combine circus skills with neurology, tells me that trying and failing sends a signal to our brain that it needs to create a new pathway. It's through the process of trying and failing that we become able to do things that we previously couldn't do. He also tells me that daily practice becomes much easier when you leave juggling balls lying around. If there's something you are finding hard to get off the ground right now, what would make it easier to pick up? Making it more visible or more bite size perhaps? Putting a baby step on your to-do list, lowering the stakes or leaving the file out to tinker with?

You never completely switch off from everything else. You're always aware of what's in the air – what could drop if another variable is introduced or someone throws you a curveball – and what, invariably, you need to come back to in order to keep in motion. There's an amount of work devoted to keeping everything going. The act of juggling itself takes effort and I guess that's the trade-off. For those of us who find ourselves playing in multiple arenas, we need to devote part of ourselves to the art and act of juggling itself. But we need to make sure that juggling is not all we do. What we juggle has to be meaningful – otherwise we run the risk of just going through the motions, exhausting ourselves just to keep all the balls in the air.

You keep moving. My son asked me a brilliant question one day, as we watched my husband park his motorbike in the garage: 'How do you stay balanced?'. The answer I realised was: you keep moving. You can't really balance on a bike standing still. And that's the thing: life isn't static. It isn't a sequence of scientific, carefully measured, uniform steps. It's expressive, passionate and full of movement – like a dance, where there's rhythm and variety.

I'm told that once you get into a rhythm, the process of juggling is actually really relaxing! Juggling can even be used as a therapy to relieve stress and anxiety and promote well-being as well as brain function. Once we find our groove and establish a rhythm, we become excited to learn new tricks and try different combinations. We become adventurous and experiment with what and how we juggle because we have a steady rhythm to come back to.

There's a limit to how many balls you can physically hold in your hand. Don't be afraid to drop a few balls (or your standards) from time to time – especially if you are picking up new ones. As much as it looks spectacular when we see circus performers juggling a great array of wonderful things, there's also a beauty in simplicity and variety. Rollercoasters can be breathtaking and brilliant fun, but they lose their appeal if we are on them all the time. I won't deny there's something exhilarating about getting to the end of a whirl-wind week, I imagine not unlike the adrenaline rush of an extreme sport. There's something incredibly life affirming about living full on and realising that we're capable of far more than we thought initially. But when exhilaration becomes exhaustion, when anticipation becomes dread, when energising becomes draining and wonder-ment becomes utter confusion, that's when I know it's time to change something – to strip back and simplify, to take life at a slower pace, to reclaim and redefine what it means to live life to the full.

At the risk of bringing another metaphor into the picture, I recently read in *Digging for Diamonds* by Cathy Madavan that diamonds shine brilliantly because they have multiple facets. If a diamond is cut with too many facets, it dulls and loses its fire. But with the right combination multiple facets create brilliance by **slowing down** the light. Yet how often do we see multiple roles as a sign that we have to speed up because we have so much to do? Juggling is exhausting when we feel we have to fulfil all our roles at the same rate, pace, depth and breadth, as if it was the only thing we do. When we allow ourselves to slow down to a pace that works for us, juggling can be a beautiful thing.

When we're juggling well, everything is separate and interlinked. One thing leads to another. When the different facets of our lives work well together, the light bounces around and lights us up brilliantly. Just as the juices from a roast chicken and the cooking water from the vegetables can come together to make a delicious gravy, when the different roles in our lives complement rather than compete with each other, there's a sense of cohesion and flow that makes life both easier and richer.

Over to you

> ## What would it take for you to juggle all that's important to you?
>
> Stop multitasking with:
>
> ....
>
> ....
>
> ....
>
> ....
>
> Allow these parts of my life to come together and support each other:
>
> ....
>
> ....
>
> ....
>
> ....
>
> I know I'm giving **my** all when I'm:
>
> ....
>
> ....
>
> ....
>
> ....
>
> To juggle well I give myself permission to
>
> let go of: ....
>
> accept: ....
>
> fully pursue: ....
>
> ask for help with: ....
>
> challenge or change: ....

TAKE YOUR TIME

'Not enough time, too much to do' is how most of our productivity conversations start.

But, when we look deeper, we find that time is not the enemy. The more we fight time, the less of it we have. If you feel like time is always running away from you, that you never seem to have enough time, if you're constantly busy, rushing round after other people, wondering when you'll ever have some time to yourself, if you are waiting for when you have more time, I have three words for you:

Take your time.

Here's why. When we don't have enough time we rush. When my daughter tries to wriggle her foot into her snug winter boots without losing her balance and my son tugs and fiddles with his laces, I find myself saying, 'It's ok, take your time.' Because if they rush it gets harder, and more frustrating, and takes longer.

When we don't have enough time we hold back or give up. What have you told yourself you'll do when you have time? What would you love to do if only you had the time? Rest, sleep, me time, read a book, write a book, take a holiday, go for a walk, upgrade the software, expand the business, take the risk, train, delegate, think, plan, prepare, go for a run, be still... So often, the things we put off are the things that would add meaning, simplicity or joy to our lives. The things that make life better and time worthwhile.

So many people wait. They wait for the work to finish, the demands to stop, the constant busyness to slow down, so they can finally have time to do what they want to do. And yet that time never comes, because the work never stops and there's always more to do.

When we don't have enough time we faff, we procrastinate, we look for distraction. Something to scratch the itch, to quell the sound of the clock ticking, to make us feel like we're doing something. Yet, often, when we just sit with it, take our time, for what might seem like forever but in reality is probably just 20 minutes, the momentum starts flowing and we get it done.

When we don't have enough time, we can miss the moments. As the saying goes, life is not measured by the number of breaths we take, but by the moments that take our breath away. When we obsess over counting the seconds, we can miss the moments. Moments of profound joy and intense silliness, roaring laughter and peaceful silence, heartwarming connection and satisfying rest. Whether it's the simple pleasures or crazy adventures, these are the moments that make life worth living. These are the moments to take our time over.

The truth is, we have time – and we choose how we spend it.

As one workshop delegate recently put it, 'If I choose to look at my work emails at the weekend and see something that upsets me, I'm the one who has chosen to let emails ruin my weekend. It's my choice, not anybody else's.' The uncomfortable truth is, if you never seem to have any time for yourself, your agenda and what matters to you, you're choosing not to give any time to yourself.

We make that choice, by what we say yes and no to, what we commit to and what we fail to commit to, what we make ourselves available for, and what we pay attention to. It's our time, to use or to give away as we choose. And the beauty is, when we stop seeing time as something that runs away without us, when we start taking our time, we choose how we experience that time.

We can't change time, but we can change our experience of it. Sometimes time flies, sometimes it drags and that's nothing to do with the seconds, minutes and hours, but everything to do with what we choose. So here's what I propose. Let's stop talking about time like there's not enough, like it's some unstoppable tsunami that we're trying to wrestle into submission.

Let's just take our time.

If you feel like life is doing you, rather than the other way round, take your time. It's yours to do as you choose. You are in control. You really are.

If you've been waiting for the perfect time that never seems to come, Take your time. It's yours, my darling. Take it, run with it, play with it, live it.

If you're dealing with new ground, ill health or challenging circumstances that mean you're not going as fast as you would like, it's ok. You're doing great. Give yourself the space. Be patient, be kind. Take your time. You'll get there.

And if you're taking time off, take it, savour it, enjoy every moment. Don't count it by seconds, measure it by moments. Enjoy every moment.

Whatever your circumstances, whatever lies before you, here's my challenge and my invitation.

Take your time.

What did you think of this book?

We're really keen to hear from you about this book, so that we can make our publishing even better.

Please log on to the following website and leave us your feedback.

It will only take a few minutes and your thoughts are invaluable to us.

www.pearsoned.co.uk/bookfeedback

NOTES AND REFERENCES

Chapter 1

1. TED, 2009. Simon Sinek: 'How great leaders inspire action'. Available at: **www.ted.com/talks/simon_sinek_how_great_leaders_inspire_action**

2. *Psychology Today*, 2013. 'The science behind the joy of sharing joy'. Available at: **www.psychologytoday.com/blog/feeling-it/201307/the-science-behind-the-joy-sharing-joy**

3. *Ibid.*

4. Steven Furtick, 2011. Speaking at the 'Willow Creek Global Leadership Summit'.

5. Lencioni, P., 2012. *The Advantage: Why Organizational Health Trumps Everything Else in Business.* Jossey-Bass: San Francisco, CA.

Chapter 2

1. Go lightly. Available at: **www.golightly.fi**

2. Allen, D., 2015. *Getting Things Done: The Art of Stress-free Productivity.* Piatkus: London.

3. Covey, S., 2004. *Seven Habits of Highly Effective People: Powerful Lessons in Personal Change.* Simon & Schuster: London.

4. Allcott, G., 2014. *How to be a Productivity Ninja: Worry Less, Achieve More and Love What You Do.* Icon Books: London.

5. Hope, K., 2015. 'Top bosses reveal their secrets for getting things done', BBC News. Available at: **http://www.bbc.co.uk/news/business-31482986**

6. Danziger, P., Levav, J. and Avnaim-Pesso, L., 2011. 'Extraneous factors in judicial decisions', *Proceedings of the National Academy of Sciences of the United States of America*. Available at: **http://www.pnas.org/content/108/17/6889**

Chapter 3

1. Urban, T., 'Why Procrastinators Procrastinate', Wait But Why. Available at: **http://waitbutwhy.com/2013/10/why-procrastinators-procrastinate.html**

2. The Pomodoro Technique. Available at: **http://pomodorotechnique.com**

3. Tracy, B., 2007. *Eat That Frog!: 21 Great Ways to Stop Procrastinating and Get More Done in Less Time*. Berrett-Koehler Publishers: Oakland, CA.

4. Irresistible Living. Available at: **www.jenniehk.com**

5. Routledge, H., 'How game thinking can boost your productivity!' Available at: **http://grace-marshall.com/how-game-thinking-can-boost-your-productivity/**

6. Warrell, M., 2014. 'Afraid of being "found out"? How to overcome imposter syndrome'. Available at: **www.forbes.com/sites/margiewarrell/2014/04/03/impostor-syndrome/**

7. McGuinness, M. 'Start small: why tinkerers get things done', *99U*. Available at: **http://99u.com/articles/19139/start-small-why-tinkerers-get-things-done**

8. Forster, M., 2006. *Do it Tomorrow and Other Secrets of Time Management*. Hodder & Stoughton: London, p. 170.

9. Paraphrased from a talk by Erwin McManus, author of *The Artisan Soul*. HarperOne: London.

Chapter 4

1. Pidgeon, E., 2014. 'The economic impact of bad meetings', TED. Available at: **http://ideas.ted.com/the-economic-impact-of-bad-meetings/**.

2. Grady, D., 2013. 'How to save the world (or at least yourself) from bad meetings', TED. Available at: **www.ted.com/talks/david_grady_how_to_save_the_world_or_at_least_yourself_from_bad_meetings**

3. Will It Make The Boat Go Faster? Olympic-winning strategies for business success. Available at: **www.willitmaketheboatgofaster.com**

4. American Psychological Association, 2010. 'Stress in America Findings'. Available at: **www.apa.org/news/press/releases/stress/2010/national-report.pdf**

5. Koven, S., 2013. 'Busy is the new sick', In Practice. Available at: **www.boston.com/lifestyle/health/blog/inpractice/2013/07/busy_is_the_new_sick.html**

6. Cambridge Dictionaries Online, definitions of 'faff about/around'. Available at: **http://dictionary.cambridge.org/dictionary/british/faff-about-around**

Chapter 5

1. The Sean Blog, 2011. 'Leave me alone!!! (using Lync to NOT communicate)'. Available at: **http://blogs.technet.com/b/seanearp/archive/2011/09/06/leave-me-alone-using-lync-to-not-communicate.aspx**

2. Dr Penny Pullan is founder of Making Projects Work Ltd, which focuses on solutions to make projects and programmes work. Available at: **http://makingprojectswork.co.uk**

3. Dr Henry Cloud is a clinical psychologist, acclaimed leadership expert and best-selling author. Available at: **http://drcloud.com**.

4. 'Margin' series, LifeChurch.tv. Available at: **www.lifechurch.tv/message-archive/watch/margin/2/message/low-res**

Chapter 6

1. Silk, D., *Loving Our Kids On Purpose*. Available at: **http://www.lovingonpurpose.com/parenting/**.

2. Saunders, E. G., 'Setting Boundaries & Saying No... Nicely'. Available at: **http://99u.com/articles/7076/setting-boundaries-saying-no-nicely**.

3. Hyatt, M., 'Using email templates to say "no" with grace'. Available at: **http://michaelhyatt.com/using-email-templates-to-say-"no"-with-grace.html**.

Chapter 7

1. Cantwell, M., 2013. *Be a Free Range Human: Escape the 9-5, Create a Life You Love and Still Pay the Bills*. Kogan Page: London. **www.beafreerangehuman.com**

2. Bradberry, T., 2015. 'Sleep Deprivation is Killing You and Your Career', research from Division of Sleep Medicine at the Harvard Medical School. Available at: **www.inc.com/travis-bradberry/sleep-deprivation-is-killing-you-and-your-career.html**

3. Gallagher, J., 2014. '"Arrogance" of ignoring need for sleep', BBC News. Available at: **www.bbc.co.uk/news/health-27286872**

4. Rock, L. and McVeigh, T. (eds.) 'It's time to stop this competitive sleep deprivation', *The Guardian*. Available at: **www.theguardian.com/theobserver/she-said/2014/may/16/its-time-to-stop-this-competitive-sleep-deprivation**

5. Widrich, L., 2012. 'How Your Productivity Is Determined by What You Eat', Buffer. Available at: **https://blog.bufferapp.com/the-science-behind-how-your-nutrition-will-decide-your-productivity-for-today**.

6. John Ratey, M.D. Available at: **www.johnratey.com**

Chapter 8

1. Arnett, G., 2013. 'Who works the most hours – MPs or teachers?', *The Guardian*. Available at: **www.theguardian.com/news/data-blog/2013/apr/23/who-works-most-teachers-or-mps**

2. Pink, D. H., 2010. 'Netflix lets it staff take as much holiday as they want whenever they want and it works', *The Telegraph*. Available at: **www.telegraph.co.uk/finance/newsbysector/mediatechnolo-gyandtelecoms/7945719/Netflix-lets-its-staff-take-as-much-holiday-as-they-want-whenever-they-want-and-it-works.html**

3. Branson, R. 'Why we're letting Virgin staff take as much holiday as they want', Virgin. Available at: **www.virgin.com/richard-branson/why-were-letting-virgin-staff-take-as-much-holiday-as-they-want**

4. Aha! Academy of High Achievers. Available at: **www.aha-success .co.uk**.

5. Bateson, K. 'Ready, steady, power pose!', *Productive Magazine!* Available at: **http://productivemag.com/28/ready-steady-power-pose#**

6. Dr Rob Archer, The Career Psychologist, **www.thecareerpsychologist .com**

Chapter 9

1. Rudd, M., Vohs, K. D. and Aaker, J., 2012. 'Awe Expands People's Perception of Time, Alters Decision Making, and Enhances Well-Being', *Psychological Science*, 23(10), pp. 1130–1136.

2. *Ibid.*

3. Greenberg, S., 2012. 'Jennifer Aaker: How to Feel Like You Have More Time', Stanford Business. Available at: **www.gsb.stanford.edu/ insights/jennifer-aaker-how-feel-you-have-more-time**

4. Rudd, M., Vohs, K. D. and Aaker, J., 2012. 'Awe Expands People's Perception of Time, Alters Decision Making, and Enhances Well-Being', *Psychological Science*, 23(10), pp. 1130–1136.

5. *Ibid.*

6. McGonigal, K., 2013. 'How to make stress your friend', TED Global. Available at: **www.ted.com/talks/kelly_mcgonigal_how_to_ make_stress_your_friend?**

Chapter 10

1. American Psychological Association, 2006. 'Multitasking: switching costs.' Available at: **www.apa.org/research/action/multitask .aspx**

2. Slaughter, A.-M., 2013. 'Can we all "have it all"?', TED Global. Available at: **www.ted.com/talks/anne_marie_slaughter_can_we_all_ have_it_all**

3. Blazoned, M., 2014. 'The Default Parent', *Huffington Post*. Available at: **www.huffingtonpost.com/m-blazoned/ the-default-parent_b_6031128.html**

INDEX